THE
WINE LOVER'S
QUIZ BOOK

THE
WINE LOVER'S QUIZ BOOK

CHALLENGING QUESTIONS & ANSWERS
FOR WINE BUFFS & BLUFFERS

PETER ADAMS

HPBooks

This book was designed and produced by
The Rainbird Publishing Group Limited
27 Wrights Lane, London W8 5TZ, England
for HPBooks, Inc., P.O. Box 5367,
Tucson, Arizona 85703 USA.

Originally published in Great Britain under the title
The Ultimate Wine Quiz Book.

Library of Congress Cataloging-in-Publication Data

Adams, Peter
    The wine lover's quiz book.

        1. Wine and winemaking.   I. Title
TP548.A224 1987   641.2'22   87-12002
ISBN 0-89586-633-1

First published in the United States of America 1987

Consultant Editor : Rosalind Cooper
Designer : Robert Mathias

Printed in Great Britain

CONTENTS

INTRODUCTION

The dinner party was in full swing. A fly on the wall would have remarked that all were enjoying themselves. The red wine was being served. The wine was certainly a great Bordeaux. This was not inspired tasting as I was very much expecting something of the sort. One of the joys of being in the wine trade is that friends so often produce their best bottle and, even nicer, the more understanding of them never require one to guess the contents.

The wine was marvellous and, above the hubbub, I asked my host what we were drinking. He replied that it was a magnum, decanted about an hour ago, Château Margaux 1934. This silenced the table. I was astounded, feeling that when someone is about to serve such a great wine, they should let their guests know and give them a chance to pause from entertaining their neighbours and take time to appreciate the claret. The rest of the company definitely agreed with me, but our host was quite insistent that he wouldn't do that for fear of acquiring the reputation of being a wine snob.

Whoever invented that emotive misnomer did great harm. Fortunately, we seem to be outgrowing the wine snob era. Today, discussing wine is accepted as one of the more pleasurable forms of conversation and invariably and increasingly crops up whatever the occasion.

Obviously, there exist wine bores (some of them monumental) but so there are golf, hunting or racing bores or just bores. Maybe there are fewer around now that discussing wine has become fun and this book hopes to join in the fun. Its format is that of a quiz with answers. It may or may not increase your knowledge of wine but it could be helpful if you get a bit lost during some wine chatter and find yourself left out. Let drop one of the questions and with any luck you are back in the race. The book tries to maintain an easy balance between the serious and less serious. Both questions and answers cover a little of the academics of wine but are still designed for easy, bedside reading, and most particularly for promoting wine discussions. It is always amusing when discussions really get going, because

sooner or later some form of gamesmanship rears its inevitable head. We like to think that gamesmanship is unsporting but we all try it and wine enthusiasts are no exception save that they may slightly disguise it by a donnish approach.

The other day, I was discussing with friends that age-old question, which wine best accompanies what food and there seemed a danger of the bores taking over. So, with the gravity of Buster Keaton one of the party asked 'Which wine goes best with offal sautés?' Obviously a joke question, well delivered and at the right time. But no, we had forgotten one of our guests had previously lived in Hungary and he replied immediately that that was an easy question as in his part of Hungary offal sautés were very popular and they usually drank with them a dry, white wine, made from the Furmint grape in the Tokay area, up in the North East. The conversation was then back on course.

It can be totally frustrating to get too involved with the various wine/food combinations. We are speaking only of quality wine, for ordinary, decent red, white or rosé wine drinks comfortably with pretty well anything.

There are no strict rules but over the years the following broad mix seems to appeal to the average person:

All fish (unless cooked in red wine). White wine.

All meat. Red wine, although white seems to go equally well with poultry and other white meats.

Cheese. Red wine wins fairly easily, but frankly wine and cheese in general make such a good partnership that many people may well prefer white.

As an aperitif. White wine without food seems far easier to get on with, than red. But if one drinks only red, then the early maturing types, possibly slightly chilled, best fill the bill.

Dessert. By tradition, in a long, formal meal, the dessert is accompanied by champagne (less dry than brut) or a sweet white still wine. These dessert wines are often of the highest quality – Sauternes, *Auslesen* German wines or late harvested wines from California or wherever. They seem rather wasted on the dessert. The habit may have arisen from the still classical pairing of a fresh peach and Sauternes. But today, an unadorned peach – or indeed an unadorned anything – is rarely served. Certainly there is nothing pleasanter than a cool, sweetish white wine to be drunk as the meal draws to a close, but preferably not actually with the dessert but afterwards.

There is a simple test anyone can try. When the dessert wine is served, before touching the dessert, taste the wine and register your opinion. Then take a mouthful of dessert followed by a second taste of the wine. Does the latter still taste the same?

Quality sweet wines today probably offer the best value of any higher quality wine – but when does one drink them? The Germans have the easiest answer – at any time except during a meal. Perhaps the truest answer is to drink sweet wines (should you feel like it) at any time; some people like them more, others less, than dry wines but all usually enjoy a change.

What everyone seems to agree but few practise is that any dessert wrecks any dry red wine. Yet people often finish off the red wine in their glass while eating some fancy dessert. It is a compliment to your host or hostess to finish your red wine before starting on the dessert. Similarly, it is stupid for a guest's glass to be re-filled with red wine once the dessert has been served.

There are a few everyday dishes which may cause problems with wine. Salad is one. Few salad dressings help any wine, but when the salad is served as a separate course there is no problem as you should drink nothing with it. Sometimes it accompanies the meat course and usually a bite of bread between salad and wine does the trick. Red or white wine goes very well with lamb but not when this is covered with mint sauce or jelly; no wine can compete against mint sauce. Asparagus is not easy. The Rheinland of Germany is a great growing area of the white variety and, at the beginning of the season, most restaurants in the area have an extra menu showing various ways of serving asparagus. They invariably drink with it a very dry, tart, white wine, although I suspect the average person while sticking to white would prefer something rounder and more buttery – maybe a Chardonnay.

Going back to an earlier part of the meal, if you are tired of the dreary water ice served as a sorbet, try a very small glass of Calvados – it is a very good cleanser.

Someone years ago coined the adage 'the grape and the grain do not mix'. It sounds euphonious and authoritative but is totally untenable. A whisky or gin is an excellent pre-dinner drink but keep it discreet. The aperitif pause before the meal often lingers on.

Frankly, we are now in danger of getting too detailed and can probably learn from the Italians. An Italian does not smell, regard and exclaim over his wine. He drinks it, and a lot of it – about 25 imperial (30 US) gallons annually per person. More important, perhaps, he knows instinctively that whatever wine is produced, it will match the home cooking.

We can discuss wine, we can think wine and (fortunately) we can drink wine. All give pleasure. Even so, the greatest pleasure probably comes from having the confidence to taste wine, knowing that you can differentiate one wine from another. Most of us have that ability, after all we taste other food and drink perfectly well, two or three times a day – why not wine? This book alas cannot make you into a skilled wine-taster (only practice will do that and genes may help) but hopefully, it might spur your endeavours.

Wine tasting seems to take two distinct forms. Firstly, the glamour exercise when one is expected to name the vineyard, vintage and total pedigree of a decanted wine. Practised by a junta of professionals in the quiet of a sample room, this may be successful. Practised in the hurly-burly of a dinner party it exposes one to appalling hazards. Even so, there are a number of people who just have to have a go and they should be admired, as long as they don't get boorish. This is not a debunking exercise, indeed it is essential in any form of tasting to concentrate on some essential aspect of the wine, be it the grape variety or the country of origin. Incidentally, if you guess these two correctly during a dinner party, you are doing exceptionally well. For those who aim for great detail, there is always the danger of entering the world of deduction. Then, when you are trying to remember which wines were served when you previously dined in the house and whether your host would be likely to serve a Bordeaux younger than 1967, you may well miss the appreciation and enjoyment of a fine wine.

Sadly I have to admit that a little tasting and a lot of deduction can produce miracles but beware, sooner or later it could land you in trouble.

The second type of wine tasting which beginners and old pros can equally enjoy is the grading of wine either on quality alone or on a balance of cost and quality. It is here you start the apprenticeship of wine appreciation which few of us ever complete.

May we now query the mass remark so often heard at wine functions – 'Of course I'm no expert but I know what I like.' The first part of the phrase may or may not be correct but if you really know what you like, it is the very essence of grading wines. Therefore ignore the mystique that still lingers on and get into the fun of tasting wines blind. You are tasting to decide your own order of merit of, say, six wines. It is almost impossible to do that accurately unless you taste blind. A simple exercise at home could be as follows. Buy six similarly priced *vins de table* from various areas – red or white. Taste them and record your order of preference. Then get some neutral to change the order and disguise the bottles. Now taste blind and then compare your findings. You will soon graduate to grading wines on a balance of cost and quality. As a suggestion, buy some wines made primarily from the Cabernet Sauvignon grape, maybe from the Médoc, from Bulgaria, California, and so on. (The prices will be very different.) Taste them blind and you could save money. Only you can teach yourself to taste; it is a totally personal exercise and you soon discover your style. A few do's and don'ts may be of help. Always have two glasses. It is easier to compare the bouquet and colour of two wines together rather than one after the other. Even at public tastings, arm yourself with two glasses as you go round the room.

Never be in a hurry actually to taste the wine. First, try and register the smell of each wine and note their shades of colour. Maybe one has a smell (bouquet) which you don't like, then leave it to the end. You can so easily pass on a foreign smell to the next glass or even imagine you have. A wine whose bouquet comes to you easily, note as a possible winner.

Colour seems to register more easily. You will soon recognize the deep red of a sound wine, and the mauve tinges which suggest youth and the tawny edges which suggest the opposite. With white wine a deep yellow may be perfectly normal but be cautious if it has tints of brown. Trying to decide your order of preference by nose and eyes before you eventually sip the wine (or take quite a mouthful, it's up to you) gets the adrenalin running – then taste. Really and totally concentrate on the difference between each pair of wines you taste. Does one have a stronger 'goodbye' than the other (in effect does the taste linger or disappear)?

Record your findings in any way you like. Complicated tasting sheets are anathema and, I believe, take your mind off the job.

Make up your own similes to describe your tastes and never fuss when you're wrong.

The great wines of Europe and California are only infallible at the very top – the expense account range. Going down the scales of quality they take their share of wins and losses. So if you happen to prefer an Israeli Cabernet to a usually more prestigious area, you may easily be right.

We hope your 'drinkatite' is now wettened sufficiently to tackle the questions and scan the answers. Should you wish to dig deeper into the answers, erudite and authoritative wine books are legion.

To make any suggestions in this respect is merely a personal choice but the fullest possible knowledge of the subject is to be found in Alexis Lichine's (*New*) *Encyclopedia of Wines and Spirits* and the *Wine Companion* by Hugh Johnson called in the US *Hugh Johnson's Modern Encyclopedia of Wine*.

Some Terms Explained	The following abbreviations and terms are used throughout the book:

AC or **AOC** — *Appellation d'Origine Contrôlée*: the finest French classification for quality wines.

DO — *Denominaciones de Origen*: the appellation awarded in Spain.

DOC — *Denominazione di Origine Controllata*: the Italian equivalent to the French AOC.

DOCG — *Denominazione di Origine Controllata e Garantita*: a recent and higher Italian Governmental classification.

QmP — *Qualitätswein mit Prädikat*: a German wine with the added classifications of quality as follows – *Kabinett, Spätlese, Auslese, Beerenauslese* or *Trockenbeerenauslese* (TBA).

VDQS — *Vin Delimité de Qualité Supérieure*: the second grade of French quality wines.

Vins de Pays — Literally, country wine. In simple terms, a *vin de table* but with a definitive geographical association.

SECTION
I

Starters

A Wine Warm-up

1. Define wine in three words.

2. Three countries regularly top the annual per capita consumption of wine. Can you name them?

3. The largest acreage of vineyards in Europe is found in which country?

4. Can you think of any connection between Worms and Mother's milk?

5. Red Bordeaux and traditional vintage port are able to mature in bottle longer than most wines, but what causes any wine to mature in bottle may not be yet fully understood. What is your explanation?

6. '*Vins de pays*' sounds right. Indeed, it sounds as French as 'mild and bitter' sounds English. But is it all a bit of a 'con' or are there meaningful regulations covering *vins de pays*?

7. (a) How many acres in a hectare?
(b) How many gallons in a hectolitre?
(c) How many gallons in a *tonneau*?

8. Cabernet d'Anjou is:
(a) The private loo of the Duke d'Anjou
(b) A rosé wine of *Kabinett* quality
(c) A rosé wine made from the Cabernet Sauvignon
(d) A rosé wine made from the Cabernet Franc
Which?

9. (a) Vinho Verde
(b) Dão

(c) Garrafeira

The above three words apply to wines of which country?

10. Where would you expect to find:
(a) Côtes de Blaye?
(b) Côtes de Bourg?

11. Within each of these areas one can find a wine of world renown. Can you name them?

(a) Aloxe-Corton	A red *grand cru*
(b) Sauternes	A white *premier grand cru*
(c) Montalcino	A DOCG
(d) Pomerol	The most expensive wine there
(e) Bernkastel	Just what the doctor ordered
(f) St Helena Napa	A female Cabernet

12. Paul gave very sound advice on wine when he wrote to Timothy. What was the advice?

13. A thousand years ago a Norse explorer discovered Vineland. Where was he?

14. Should all wine with a cork closure be stored in the horizontal position?

15. There is Beaujolais Primeur, Muscadet Primeur (see photograph) and at least one other major French contender in this lucrative market for new wine. Can you name the other wine? And in which month are they all released?

16. What is the first essential of the temperature at which bottled wines may be stored?

Answers on page 22   13

II

Grapes and All That

1. Name the odd man out: Lambrusco; Vinifera; Labrusca.

2. Nowhere in France is the AOC given to the grape variety, it is always geographical. But in Brittany, the rule seems to be broken, or does it? Can you elucidate?

3. Riesling is the principal grape of which German wine-producing areas?

4. Name the odd man out: Cabernet, Merlot, Malbec, Cérons and Cinsault.

5. Varietal labels are becoming increasingly popular world-wide. In France what *appellation* would one expect to see on the labels of the following wines?
    (a) An Alsace Riesling
    (b) A Chardonnay from the Maconnais
    (c) A Gamay from the Loire

6. Recently, tasting white Hermitage in the cellars of a farmer at Tain l'Hermitage, I enquired (in the hope that he would think I knew the form) what the percentage was of Marsanne and Rousanne grapes in his blend. He looked at me as if I'd come from outer space and replied, 'We gave up using — grape, years ago.'
    Which grape had he given up using and why?

7. A cross of the following grape varieties makes up two popular and fairly recent German grapes:
    (a) Riesling and Trollinger (red)
    (b) Silvaner and Weisser Burgunder (Pinot Blanc)
The names of the two grapes please.

8. There is a rather splendid word 'ampelography' which

in simple terms means the identification of vines. Rightly or wrongly a number of the following grapes are said to be the same; can you match them up?

Trebbiano; Steen; Melon de Bourgogne; St Emilion; Chenin Blanc; Muscadet; Pineau de Loire; Ugni Blanc.

Incidentally (and a complete *non-sequitur*), there is an equally splendid and similar word 'ampelotherapy' meaning the treatment of illness with grapes, hopefully in their fermented form. Experience suggests this word has not yet reached the medical profession.

9. Ignoring Ahr and Wurttemberg, two grape varieties dominate the viticulture of the other nine main German wine areas (*Anbaugebiete*). Do you know:
(a) Their names
(b) Which grape is dominant in Rheinhessen
(c) Which grape dominates the Mittelrhein.

10. The grape varieties Tempranillo Red and Viura White are popular
(a) In which European country?
(b) By which French grape names are they known?

11. Is there a common denominator between Sancerre, Reuilly, Quincy and Pouilly-Fumé?

12. The white grape Tocai or Tokay is found in many parts of Europe.
(a) In Italy, which is perhaps the most successful Tocai?
(b) In Germany, it is called what?
(c) In Alsace, it has an alternative name, what is it?
(d) Which Hungarian grape is used in Tokaji Aszu?

13. These three grape types are not quite what they seem –

where are they grown and what style of wine do they yield?

   (a) Golden Chasselas
   (b) Emerald Riesling
   (c) Grey Riesling

14. The University of California at Davis has defined five types of region for grape-growing numbered I to V. Which is comparable to German winemaking conditions – region I or region V – and can you indicate where it might be on the attached map of the San Francisco Bay Area?

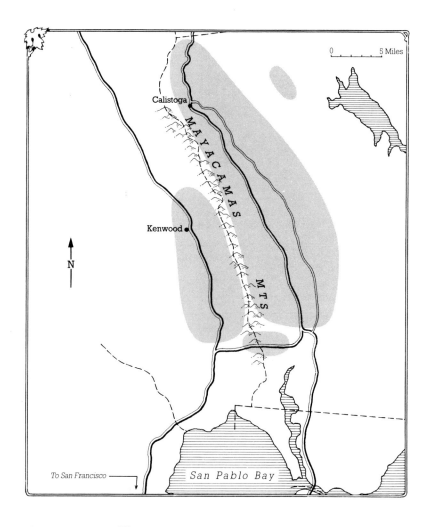

Answers on page 27

III

Joy in the Making

1. Gospel of St Mark, Chapter 2, Verse 22: 'And no man putteth new wine into old bottles ...'. Why?

2. The *solera* system is:
   (a) The use of the sun's rays to help flash pasteurization
   (b) The warming of outside thermal vats in north Rioja
   (c) A method of maturing Spanish sherry.
Which is correct?

3. What do you understand by malolactic fermentation?

4. In the opinion of many German winemakers, *Süssreserve* surpasses sulphur. Can you explain?

5. At some stage during the fermentation of Portuguese port, brandy is added to the fermenting must. Is this to increase the alcohol or the sweetness of the resulting wine?

6. *Macération carbonique* – which has the sinister ring of some medieval punishment, but is in fact a way of dealing with young wines, not young offenders. Can you explain it all more fully?

7. All Spanish sherries are fermented right through to be dry wines, except those destined for the 'cream market' whose fermentation is stopped by the addition of Spanish brandy to maintain some sugar in the wine. True or false?

8. Calamus, camomile, cinnamon and cloves all help to flavour what?

9. Pink Chablis in northern Burgundy is made with the Pinot Noir grape, but vinified white. True or false?

10. Chaptalization or, in Germany, gallization is which of the following?
- (a) The head or cap of pulp (skins, etc.), which rises to the top of a fermenting vat of red wine.
- (b) The addition of sugar to sugar-deficient wines.

11. One does not press black grapes to make red wine but only white grapes to make white wine. True or false?

12. Match the firm/owner/personality associated with the following wines:
- (a) Hearty Burgundy
- (b) Bernkasteler Doktor
- (c) Tignanello
- (d) Quinta de Vargellas
- (e) Taltarni
- (f) Gran Coronas Reserva
- (g) Château d'Angludet
- (h) Laborie

13. Where is a quality brandy made by Brothers?

14. Wine vats and presses beneath – why should they be arranged like this?

1. This is a sneaky, trick question – beware. The majority of Rhein wines are bottled in brown bottles, while the majority of wines from the Mosel are bottled in green bottles. We know there are exceptions – large size bottles, crock bottles, blue coloured bottles from the Nahe, and so on. But the majority rule still applies, except for one class of Rhein wine which is invariably bottled in green bottles. Which is it?

2. What are the reasons for decanting a bottle of red wine? (Conscientious objectors to all decanting are excused this question.)

Table Manners

3. Many restaurants have their red wines (whether the bottle contains sediment or not) served from a bottle cradled in a wine basket. Do you agree this lessens the chance of the sediment entering the customer's glass?

4. Which wine should one drink with grapes?

5. 'Don't put your daughter on the stage Mrs Worthington, and don't put your red wine on the ice ...'. No, Noel Coward did not quite say that, but would he have been wrong to have said the latter half?

6. Urgent query heard in the wine shop: 'My husband's boss is coming to dinner and I've planned it entirely "Italiano". Now I'm told we must serve a classed French wine; isn't it possible to get away with an Italian wine?'

7. She ordered oysters, and you wanted to impress with your knowledge of wine, but momentarily the name of the wine escaped you. You knew it came from around Brittany and the name was something like Muscat but not exactly. Finally, you ordered Muscat d'Alsace and got away with it. Needless to say, as you left the restaurant, the wine you had been trying to remember came to you. Which one was it?

8. Last night we stuck to the Rheingau, Riesling with the fish and a red with the meat. Is this possible?

9. I share an office with Jones known in the department as 'Old Vino'. We both belong to a pretty fancy French Dining Club but cannot always manage to attend their dinners together. Such was the form last Tuesday, and on Wednesday morning Vino could not resist elaborating on all the wines he had sampled the previous evening, before he resumed earning a living. He was still perhaps under the influence of Alka-Seltzer, voluble but not totally accurate. I thought I spotted an obvious error or two. Can you notice any?

The conversation was something like this:

VINO   Before dinner we had lashings of champagne rosé but actually, when the guy took the napkin off, it wasn't champagne but sparkling Vouvray rosé.

I   Didn't the taste tell you anything?

VINO   Shut up! With the soup, they served a *manzanilla* sherry. It was explained that the wine had spent its life in wood in the *bodegas* of Jerez de la Frontera under the floor – I didn't understand that.

I   It means under *flor*.

VINO   That's what I said. You're making this sound like a music hall duo.

    Anyway, there followed a great white Burgundy no less than a white Vougeot 1978. Then came the inevitable *foie gras*.

I   Served with Sauternes no doubt.

VINO   No, actually a rather splendid, very sweet Graves.

I   Surprise! Surprise!

VINO   Two clarets followed with the roast, Château Petrus 1975 and Château Mouton Rothschild *premier grand cru* 1970. You know, that wonderful stink of Cabernet Sauvignon from each wine seemed to fill the room. Rather curiously, there was an old chap on my right who murmured, 'Why do they serve us wines way over the hill,' and damn me, a similar type on my left sighed 'Alas! I'll never live to enjoy these wines at their best.'

I   My money's on the left-hand corner.

VINO   We ended with an Alsatian Gewürztraminer 1983 late harvested, you know *vendange tardive*. Incredibly rich but totally balanced by the fruity Gewurziness – great stuff.

I   What was the dessert?

VINO   Nothing very exciting, just a fresh peach.

10. Why does one try to compare Bordeaux and Burgundy?

11. He couldn't believe his eyes, the wine list showed Château Lafite (admittedly spelt wrong with two 't's) at a price he felt he could afford. When the wine arrived, the label made clear to him the obvious mistake he had made. But he managed to keep it hidden and she revelled in (as she thought) drinking Château Lafite for the first time. Poor chap, he can never afford to take her out again. Have you guessed the wine they were drinking?

12. Should a wine glass suit your table arrangement or the wine you will be drinking?

13. An unconventional serving method (see photograph) gains admirers – what is the name of the artist pouring the wine?

Answers on page 46

I

A Wine Warm-Up

1. Fermented grape juice. Ripe grapes have a certain bloom on the outside skin formed by natural yeasts. When the skin breaks, these yeasts feed on the sugar in the pulp of the grape producing ethyl alcohol and carbon dioxide. This is the action of fermentation which makes wine in its simplest form. From now on, whatever the oenologist, chemist, analyst or winemaker (so often one and the same person) do to that action is for the better – hopefully.

Wine as we require it today does not appear in a totally natural way nor is it merely the result of chemistry. The modern winemaker nurses and helps along nature, literally from the grape to the glass. As a result, bad wine is today the exception.

Perhaps we have been a little autocratic suggesting it is only grapes that make wine. Many of us may have made deliciously over-strong wine from parsnips, dandelions or whatever. Traditionally, such wines are referred to with a mention of the product concerned. The most common probably being apple wine, called cider in many countries.

2. Italy, France and Portugal – the order of precedence varies. The actual gallonage drunk per person varies even more. A very rough estimate is 30 imperial (36 US) gallons annually, which works out at a half-bottle per day for 360 days – surely not a difficult target!

3. One immediately thinks of Italy or possibly France, but in fact it is Spain. However, the Spanish average wine production per acre is about half the EEC norm.

Spain has its own *appellation* laws approximating to France and Italy – the *Denominaciones de Origen* (known as DO) – which have been widely given. It also now has a foothold in the export markets for table wines. Rioja dominates as traditional, and Penedes (thanks to the Torres family) as exciting and different. Whether their low yield will modernize itself, time will tell.

4. Worms is a flourishing (today, modern) town in the Rheinhessen. A few years before World War I, an over-

enthusiastic mayor of Worms was so enamoured of the wines from the Liebfrauenkirche's vineyards surrounding his local church that he declared all quality wines of Rheinhessen could call themselves Liebfraumilch. The vines still surround the same church, their name is still Liebfrauenstift and their major owner Langenbach and Co. Today, Liebfraumilch since 1971 must be a *Qualitätswein* from one *Anbaugebiet,* the latter is usually Rheinhessen, Rheinpfalz or Nahe and this area of production must be shown on the label. But why does everyone 'knock' Liebfraumilch? The thought that popularity means mediocrity surely ignores the classics, whether books, music, paintings or whatever.

5. For wines to mature, there has to be air. We know that wines in casks mature by oxidization through the staves of the cask. We also know that it is impossible to cork up a bottle of wine without air entering the bottle. Once in bottle, it is thought that the wine matures as the various elements that make up the wine themselves grow older, and the air in the bottle is sufficient. It is impossible for air to enter via the cork so long as the cork has not thinned out and the bottle is stored horizontally with the cork in contact with the wine. It is even more impossible for air to enter a vintage port bottle as the cork is often sealed with wax. Owners of the first growth châteaux in the Médoc recork their wine every 20–25 years against the danger of the corks thinning out and air entering the bottles.

6. It is certainly not a 'con'. Many people have appreciated that as they have driven across France they met regional menus and perhaps did not realize, more often than not, that they also met changing regional wines – because almost invariably they drank the house wine, in a Pichet or similar. During the early 1970s, someone attached to the French Ministry of Agriculture thought it wrong not to give some identity to the mass of wines all over France which basically had a regional message, but had not yet gained their AOC or even VDQS.

Thus, the *vins de pays* were born. They are all strictly regulated and pretasted. Basically the laws that allow *vin de pays* are based on the requirements of both AOC and

VDQS wines without being so detailed. But first and foremost they will show the delimited area from which they come. In effect, they come from Departments covering almost the whole of France, with Languedoc and Roussillon being easily the largest suppliers. A minor word of warning: don't think you have made a mistake if, having chosen a *vin de pays*, you find it is also labelled *vin de table*. The latter is required by some quirky EEC regulation.

7. (a) One hectare = 2.47 acres
   (b) One hectolitre = 100 litres = 22 imperial gallons = 26.42 US gallons
   (c) One *tonneau* = 4 *barriques* = 192 imperial gallons = 230.58 US gallons = 96 dozen bottles

These are not idle figures, but arise daily in wine affairs. Vineyards are measured in hectares. The *rendement,* which is the harvest from any one vineyard, is expressed as hectolitres per hectare. *Vin ordinaire* in bulk is usually sold at a price per hectolitre, while bulk Bordeaux is usually sold per four *barriques* for which the ancient word *tonneau* is used.

8. A rosé wine made in Anjou of Cabernet Franc or Sauvignon or both.

9. Portugal.
(a) Portugal produces appreciably more red than white wine, but one suspects their export markets associate Vinho Verde with white wine. I cannot recall seeing a Vinho Verde red wine outside Portugal. As we are talking colours, *verde* means green and Vinho Verde is exactly that, in the sense of extreme youth. The area of production is south of the river Minho in north-west Portugal. It is a highly cultivated part of the world and one sees the vines growing high on trellises allowing other crops to flourish on the ground. The locals like their wines treble fresh and still with signs of fermentation causing a prickly taste on the tongue.

   Their export models are usually softened up and even bottled medium dry.
(b) Most of Portugal produces wine but, of the red wines of controlled *appellation*, probably Dão is the best known.

A lesser claim to fame is that to the English-speaking ear it sounds like 'Dong'. The area is just south of the Douro valley, so many vineyards are terraced.

Their red wines which, as everywhere in the country, are far more numerous than the white, have a reputation for a softness reminiscent of Burgundy/Rhône, and white grapes are often included in the vinification. The white Dão, a fairly stern dry wine, is very much on the increase. (c) Garrafeira are wines considered by their producers as the firm's 'showpiece'. The blends of Garrafeira reds are the best buys in Portugal. They have been long matured in wood, but also in bottle before being released on the market.

10. They are both *appellations* of Bordeaux.
(a) Côtes de Blaye and Premières Côtes de Blaye make pleasant enough white and red wines (reputedly better red) on the other side of the river Gironde. The opposite side to the Médoc – about 50 km from Bordeaux.
(b) Côtes de Bourg is south of Blaye, making mostly red wine.

11. (a) Le Corton   (d) Château Petrus
    (b) Château Yquem   (e) Bernkasteler Doktor
    (c) Brunello di Montalcino   (f) Martha's Vineyard

12. 'Drink no longer water, but use a little wine for thy stomach's sake and thine often infirmities.'
1 Timothy, Chapter 5, Verse 23.

13. Vineland, or Vinland as some early maps have it, was the continent of America as seen by Leif Ericson. Wild vines bearing grapes flourished everywhere and indeed there are still more species of grape growing wild in America than anywhere else on earth. The borders of the United States extend from 49° latitude in Washington State to 25° latitude in Texas and Florida. All of the world's most celebrated growing regions are within these parallels but of course the acreage available to the Americans is vastly superior (for example, Champagne and Burgundy are at 49° latitude). Wines are indeed made seriously in dozens of states but the major production is centred on

California with another centre around the Finger Lakes area north of New York and an increasing output of quality wines from Oregon and Washington in the Pacific North West.

14. Emphatically 'yes'. A cork will dry out and become thinner unless kept damp by being in contact with the wine. Once the cork begins to narrow, air will enter the bottle and the wine will die. There is an argument that port in a corked bottle (and presumably any other corked fortified wine) is better stored upright as the strength of the wine is detrimental to the cork if the two are in contact – doubt it.

In a wine store many of the wines are displayed in the upright position and even those binned may be at an angle that scarcely allows the cork and wine to meet. Obviously, every wine store has the problem of proper display and correct horizontal binning, but the wines standing up are usually quick movers and therefore will not suffer.

15. The other wine is Côtes du Rhône Primeur, a respectable alternative to the Beaujolais version, and also made by the carbonic maceration method which preserves maximum fruit. These three wines are each released in November following the vintage. New Beaujolais can be described either as Nouveau or Primeur and although the latter word is strictly more correct the public seem to prefer Nouveau.

16. It is essential that there is not an appreciable rise or fall in temperature as the weather changes. This is far more important than the actual temperature of the storage place, be it cellar, spare room or cupboard. The usual 'book' answer to the ideal constant temperature is a fairly wide range, say 10°–18°Celsius. Dampness need not be an issue as long as there is a flow of air. Dampness and no draught can create mould which may attack the corks and certainly the labels if the wines are binned.

As books reputedly 'furnish' a room, so wine racks can look attractive forming a wall or partition in the dining room. However, it may be wise to divorce the heating of the room from the general central heating of the house.

II

Grapes and All That

1. The odd man out is Lambrusco, an Italian grape which appears as red, white or rosé wine, still or semi-sparkling (*frizzante*), all over Italy. Its true home is Emilia-Romagna where there are several *appellation* wines (DOC) made primarily from the Lambrusco, notably:

> Lambrusco Grasparossa di Castelvetro
> Lambrusco Salamino di Santa Croce
> Lambrusco di Sorbara

Financially, it must be one of the most successful Italian grapes and heads the range of imported wines to the USA. In Italy these wines are usually dry (they may be exported sweeter), red and fizzy. They are taken extremely seriously by the gourmets of Bologna and Modena, but for many they are an acquired taste.

At a luncheon party in a supreme restaurant in Modena our host served only Lambrusco (Castelvetro, I think). One physically longed for a great Italian wine to match this specialist cuisine (which to our host was exactly what it was doing). Anyhow, to my shame, I tipped one glass into a nearby potted plant. Alas, it was summer, the earth in the pot solid and the Castelvetro continued to fizz even more joyously than when in the glass. The courtesy with which a fine old red wine appeared could only happen in Italy.

Vinifera and *labrusca* are not grape varieties. They each represent a family of grapes originally totally unrelated.

Vitis vinifera is of European origin, has been exported all over the world and includes in its family, without exception, all the noble grapes (and many others) of the recognized wine world such as Cabernet Sauvignon, Pinot Noir, Riesling and Chardonnay.

Vitis labrusca is a native American family covering a host of individual grapes which, if used unblended, give off a so-called 'foxy' taste unacceptable to most drinkers. On country walks, I have smelt down fox-holes but have never been reminded of *labrusca*.

For many years now, the highly skilled oenologists of North America have realized that making table wine without *vinifera* grapes or with straight *labrusca* is like boxing with one arm behind one's back. They have therefore produced hybrids of French *vinifera* and American local vines, always getting closer to the *vinifera* taste and smell.

Certain areas of the wine-producing world, notably Eastern USA and Canada, cannot as yet, owing to their climate, produce *vinifera* grapes in commercial quantities. Yet even in these areas, specialized wineries dedicated to the *vinifera* grapes are producing limited quantities of fully acceptable wine. The winemakers there carry on (perfectly aware that they may lose their total crop of *vinifera* vines in any winter) because they know, sooner or later, the oenologists will come up with a *vinifera* grape 'closer' to the toughness of a *labrusca*.

Wines from the native American vines may not top the bids in the world's auction houses but a century or so ago they saved the world's vineyards, and continue to protect them today. *Phylloxera*, a parasitic louse, attacked the roots of the European vines and caused near-total destruction between 1850 and 1870, any cure seemed totally remote.

Eventually *phylloxera* was found to have entered France on American vine stocks although these vine stocks were themselves immune to it. The cure which is now a total preventative was, and still is, to graft the *vinifera* vine on to resistant American root stocks. The *vinifera* quality is apparently not affected, although the longevity of the wine is probably lessened.

2. Muscadet is a grape variety which produces a wine of the same name. One can argue that the grape Muscadet is really the old 'Melon de Bourgogne' and Muscadet is a local area. One can also argue (probably with more conviction) that today the grape is Muscadet and the area Pays Nantais. Brittany, along the Atlantic coast of northern France, produces some of the country's finest seafood and it is almost uncanny that on its doorstep it has the ideal wine with which to wash it down. Sanlucar de Barrameda in Andalucia can make a similar claim with its *manzanilla* and *langostinas*. But Muscadet has now grown up. It is no longer exclusive to the Breton. It is to be found on all the wine lists of the world, and is surely considered more as an affordable, all-purpose white wine than one that must be drunk with *'fruits de mer'*. But beware, the wine is dry, very dry – green-dry in poor years but fruity dry and most enjoyable in the riper years.

It carries three *appellations* usually in the following order of quality:

3rd   Muscadet des Coteaux de la Loire
2nd   Muscadet
1st   Muscadet de Sèvre et Maine

Any of these wines may be bottled from the barrel in which they were fermented, leaving their natural deposit in the barrel – a system to accentuate the freshness of the wine. They may then be labelled *'mise sur lie'*. The rules of *'mise sur lie'* are wide, contradictory and much debated by the local winemakers.

Perhaps the public are better advised to forget that the words denote a special type of bottling and assume they mean extra quality which in practice they invariably do.

Some of the greatest Muscadet cellars are to be found in Vallet, but the trick is to find Vallet. It is in fact situated on road D 756.

3. Rheingau and Mosel-Saar-Ruwer.

4. Cabernet Sauvignon or Franc are world-wide grapes born in Bordeaux (or so I've always assumed). The same remarks apply to Merlot. Malbec is still to be found in Bordeaux, but is much more the grape of Cahors where it is known as Cot. Cinsault is also a southern French grape, associated primarily with the Rhône valley and Provence.

Cérons is the odd man out, as it is an area, and wine, south of Graves and immediately north of Barsac. The grapes are the usual Sauternes/Barsac combination and the wine can be vinified dry as AC Graves or *'moelleux'* as AC Cérons.

5. (a) *Appellation Alsace contrôlée*
  (b) *Appellation Mâcon* or *Pinot Chardonnay Mâcon con-
     trôlée*
  (c) *Vin de pays, Vin de table*

6. Rousanne had been given up as it matured appreciably later than Marsanne.

I asked our friend if this was general throughout the area, his answer was a smile and a shrug of the shoulders which perhaps meant yes. The northern Rhône is a happy hunting ground for the wine amateur (means 'lover') but for the moment let us stay with white wine. The Viognier grape has an enormous reputation for producing white wine in its own right apart from softening red wine. Condrieu is possibly one of the great white wines of the world. It is difficult to review Château Grillet (100 per cent Viognier), as I've tasted it so rarely, but one can only admire an estate of five or six acres which has achieved its own *appellation*; the only château in France to have done so.

Yet, in a straight fight between Condrieu and white Hermitage, I have to back Hermitage.

7. (a) Kerner
(b) Morio-Muskat

8. The matches are:
i. Muscadet and Melon de Bourgogne. In the Pays Nantais, Muscadet is used exclusively. For the oddish AOC Bourgogne Ordinaire (white) the Melon de Bourgogne is a permitted grape.
ii. Trebbiano, St Emilion and Ugni Blanc. Trebbiano is a white grape in use throughout Italy. Ugni Blanc is very closely associated with Cognac, where the particular variety used is called St Emilion. Ugni Blanc, or variations of, produces dry white wines the world over.
iii. In South Africa where grape varieties are called 'cultivars', Steen is their name for Chenin Blanc. The similar '*stein*' is not a grape but a type of wine. In South Africa it can be anything; a good bet is a blend of Steen and Colombard. In Franconia, Germany, the wines are called *stein* to reflect the flat *Bocksbeutels*, commonly in use. Chenin Blanc and Pineau de Loire seem interchangeable names for the white grape primarily of Anjou and Touraine in the Loire valley.

9. (a) Müller-Thurgau and Riesling

(b) Müller-Thurgau
(c) Riesling

10. (a) Spain
   (b) Pinot Noir and Sauvignon Blanc

11. Anyone who answers 'Yes, the common denominator is the Sauvignon Blanc grape' is only half right. The white wines from the areas concerned are made exclusively from the Sauvignon, but Sancerre, Reuilly and even a little at Quincy produce red and/or rosé wines from the Pinot Noir.

Sancerre is an interesting, small hill-top town at the extreme eastern edge of the Loire area. Even since the 1950s it seems to have attracted a 'chic' image, first for its whites, then its rosés and now certainly its reds. For so small a vineyard to have achieved a bull's eye in all three colours must be unique.

The tourist usually approaches the Loire via Brittany and then drives east, against the flow of the river, knowing there is about 400 kilometres which offers an endless variety of wines. It is a great and daunting feeling. Every spring, a small group of us cheat. We drive less than 100 km and stay in a very special hotel whose wine list offers every Loire wine one has ever heard of and quite a number that one has not. Each luncheon and dinner we make an imaginary drive up and down La Loire and indeed Le Loir (never leave out Jasnières) comparing the various wines and their makers. The aperitif is usually a Crémant, Vouvray or possibly Gros Plant with a touch of Cassis. For the dry whites it can be interesting trying to match up a Sauvignon against a Chenin Blanc. There is a wide choice of Sauvignon, Reuilly, Quincy and of course Pouilly-Fumé and Sancerre, but the dry Chenin Blanc is thin on the ground with the growths of Savennières taking first place (in a good year), but a really dry Vouvray is the more unusual. Dessert wines abound – there really is a great choice: Bonnezeaux, Quarts de Chaume and some of the old Vouvrays. We usually drink them on their own, but many people seem to find desserts to match.

The old adage, 'The first duty of any wine is to be red', hardly applies in the Loire. The knowing locals seem to go for Chinon or Bourgueil (often from the ice bucket) we rather stick to Saumur-Champigny. Now for one of those remarks which is bound to be shot down. The Chenin Blanc is capable of long-time ageing in this area, but not the Sauvignon Blanc.

12. (a) Tocai Friulano, whose home base is the province of Friuli–Venezia–Giulia lying in the extreme north-east of Italy, facing Austria and Yugoslavia. Udine is the enchanting capital town, reminding one of a mini Verona. The province is an outpost of Italy and much military is stationed there.

If you notice on a wine list an Italian wine made from Tocai Friulano, notably from Collio or Gorizia or the town of Lison, order it.

(b) In Germany, it is called Rulander and is a direct relation of the Burgundy Pinot. It is mostly found in the Baden area.

(c) The Tokay d'Alsace (again a direct descendant of the Burgundy Grey Pinot) is one of the noble grapes authorized to have the *appellation* Alsace. Recently one has been allowed to label the wine Tokay or Pinot Gris or both together. It is usually a fruity wine but totally dry. Perhaps Pinot Gris has a drier message to the public than Tokay. Tokay d'Alsace is the wine that often accompanies one of the great Alsatian specialities – *foie gras*.

It is almost impossible for a visiting wine merchant to be hungry in France, but on this particular day everything had gone wrong. In the morning we had asked our host to skip lunch and perhaps serve some light snack during the tasting session. To our astonishment and, at the time, delight, he had done just that. We then had a longish drive to Alsace and, thanks to rain, a puncture and my wife's map-reading (vehemently denied) we arrived at our hotel around 11.30 p.m. – famished. We asked about the possibility of a sandwich or something, and the owner suggested soup and *foie gras* with Tokay 1976. It was hardly a meal but, nevertheless, one we will always remember – maybe 'hunger is the most piquant of sauces'.

(d) Of course the fabulous Hungarian dessert wine Tokay or Essencia of Tokay (English spelling) is not made of the Tokay grape at all. Here, Tokay is both a method of wine-

PRODUCE OF HUNGARY

50 cl

TOKAJI ASZÚ ESSENCIA

BOTTLED BY TOKAJHEGYALJA STATE WINERY, TOLCSVA.

EXPORT   MONIMPEX

IMPORTED BY
Colman's

CARROW   NORWICH

A handsome label from a bottle of Essencia of Tokay – note the half litre contents.

Edelfäule – noble rot – on grapes destined for Auslesen wine.

making and an area in far north-eastern Hungary within spitting distance of Russia, but one is more apt to swallow than spit in that part of the world. King Stephen is reputed to have described Tokaji Aszu (Hungarian spelling) as the 'King of wines and wine of kings'. It isn't a particularly original remark and had surely been said years previously by Charlemagne about Burgundy. Yet Tokay at its best is one of the great wines of the world, ranking with *Auslesen* of Germany and the top wines of Sauternes. It also defies the normal rules of wine, thriving on oxidation and remaining unspoiled for years on ullage.

Briefly the form is as follows: the only grapes allowed to be used are the Furmint, Hárslevelü and Muscat Ottonel each of which in this area, in a suitable year, are affected by noble rot, known in Sauternes as *pourriture noble*, in Germany as *Edelfäule* and in the laboratory, *Botrytis cinerea*. From the 'rotten' bunches of grapes, the most nobly rotten individual berries are picked which are known as *aszu*. These *aszu* grapes are pounded into pulp and stored in casks of 7 imperial (8.4 US) gallons known as *puttonyos*. These *puttonyos* are then added in varying proportions to one-year-old wine. This basic wine is stored in barrels of 35 imperial (42 US) gallons known as *gönci*. The *gönci* themselves are positioned in single rows

Some bottles of Tokay covered in Cladosporium cellare.

in the very narrowest of cellars. An essential part of the Tokay system is that the cellar walls are covered with *Cladosporium cellare* – mildew.

The quality of Tokay Aszu is determined by the percentage of *aszu* blended with the basic wine, and the blend remains in casks for years. Thus is produced a highly maderized rich golden drink, about 14 per cent alcohol and with 120 grams of sugar per litre.

For Kings and Commissars, there is Essencia of Tokay which one is told is the fermented juice of *aszu* only. All Tokay Aszu states on the label the number of *puttonyos* of *aszu* which have gone into the making of the wine. Five *puttonyos* is probably the highest quality before Essencia.

For lesser mortals, there is Tokay Szamorodni which contains no *aszu*. In the years when the noble rot is advanced, these wines are sweet, in poor years they are semi-sweet. Equally they can be vinified dry, by picking the grapes early before the *Botrytis* has started.

All Tokay, by tradition, is bottled in long-necked half-litre bottles only. This must put Essencia among the highest priced wines in the world.

13. All three are grown in California and produce white wines.
(a) Golden Chasselas is known as Palomino in Europe and is the principal variety for sherry-making. In California it is a 'varietal' wine of limited character which may be dry or semi-sweet. It is not related to the Chasselas grown in France.
(b) Emerald Riesling is a grape developed by the University of California at Davis by crossing Johannisberg Riesling with Muscadelle. It tends to be slightly sweet and 'flowery' on the palate. Paul Masson is the best-known producer.
(c) Grey Riesling is not a Riesling at all but a grape called Chauche Gris in France. It yields a light medium-dry wine which is perfect with a San Francisco meal of crab, salad and sourdough bread. Wente Brothers is the most familiar label.

14. Region I is the coolest for grape-growing and the area near San Francisco which rates as cool is Carneros, an area

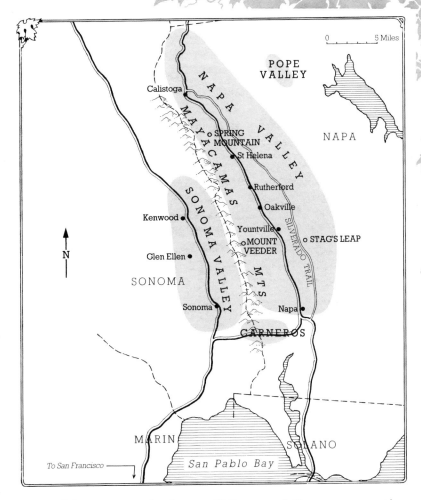

stretching across the base of Napa and Sonoma counties, cooled by fog from the bay. The most successful grape varieties here are Chardonnay, Johannisberg Riesling, Gewürztraminer and Pinot Noir. Another notable 'region I' area is Monterey County to the south of the Bay Area.

III

Joy in the Making

1. The verse continues, 'else the new wine does burst the bottles'. The word bottles obviously does not refer to glass but the quotation proves wine behaved then as now. The

Sherry quietly maturing in a solera.

violence of the initial fermentation would have burst an old, used container.

2. The answer is (c), Spanish sherry is matured by the *solera* system. It may be easier to explain what the *solera* system is not, before trying to explain what it is. It has no meaning at all which might denote the age or quality of the wine. All sherries are *solera* sherries.

Sherry is matured in oakwood and commercial sherries, even the most prestigious, do not improve in the bottle. They will change their style which possibly one may prefer, but ideally (which is obviously impossible) sherry should be served from the cask to the glass.

After the young wines (each of one harvest) have been classified, they are allotted to a *solera* which houses the type of sherry they happen to be; in the simplest form *olorosos* or *finos*.

A *solera* is a stock of butts from which wine is drawn two or three times a year. It is then replenished with the same amount of younger wine. This younger wine takes on all the characteristics of the greater amount of older wine, thus both the style and quality of the older wine continues.

The *solera* (if you like, the 'end product') is fed by a series of other stocks of butts and the refilling process goes on right down the line. These other butts (there may be any number) are the nursery (*criadera*) to the *solera*. They progressively feed each other till the final *criaderas* feed the *solera*.

Just to make things easy, all the *criaderas* plus the final stock of butts (the *solera*) will be referred to as *a solera!*

A *solera* started in 1887 does not produce a hundred-year-old wine today, but has (or could have) produced the same style of wine for the last hundred years.

Outside the sherry area, the English are assumed to be the greatest judges of sherry quality. I often wonder whether that is so. My suspicion is that the English take sherry for granted as the French accept their '*vin ordinaire*'. We like it dry or not dry, but in either case are not looking for an old *oloroso* or a *fino* the colour of mahogany – such wines, which often seem like essence of sherry and whose smells reek through the room, can only be served in Jerez with incredible *hors d'oeuvres* and give enormous delight. Frankly, they are too complicated to be the aperitif served on return from the office or before dinner.

3. This is the second fermentation which follows the main fermentation at varying periods. It can in fact be brought forward if the winemaker wants. It has the effect of changing the malic acid into the milder lactic acid and of course produces carbon dioxide.

Occasionally one comes across red wine which has been bottled before the second fermentation was totally complete. The wine may well be bright, but there will be a noticeable tingle on the tongue which decanting usually gets rid of.

4. Most exported German wines tend to sweetness. Their charm lies in the balance of sugar and acidity. Up to the early sixties, the normal method of achieving a balanced medium sweetness was to halt the fermentation, leaving some residual sugar in the wine. Fermentation was normally stopped by the addition of sulphur which could result in an unbalanced wine and possibly a smell and taste of sulphur. Modern technology then came up with a totally new route to achieve the same objective – and more accurately. When a wine is to be sweetened it can now be done by the addition of unfermented grape-juice. In the simplest terms, let us assume one is making wine X. Ninety per cent of the must would be fermented right through and wine X would be a totally dry wine. The remaining 10 per cent of the must would be stored in sterile tanks, unfermented. Before bottling, this sweet grape-juice is added to the wine in whatever proportions the winemaker judges best to produce a balanced wine. To add grape-juice to wine without creating a second fermentation is quite a technical trick, but today is commonplace.

5. Perhaps the question is slightly misleading. If you add brandy to any liquid, it must increase the alcohol, but in the production of port that is not the purpose of the exercise. Brandy is added during fermentation to stop that fermentation (the ferments are killed at around 16 per cent alcohol) and so preserve unfermented grape sugar in the wine. Again the wording is misleading as the fermenting juice is usually added to the brandy. Well before fermentation is complete, the fermenting juice is pumped into vats/barrels containing a measure of brandy, and fermentation ceases. One is then left with a young wine of natural sweetness.

6. We know, of course, what it is all about, but on the whole would prefer not having to explain it. First of all, one has the shock of finding out that the lucky old grape can have a second form of fermentation. This second form operates actually inside the grape itself, and takes colour and fruit from the inner skin. It can only happen in an oxygen-free vat or whatever, sealed with carbon dioxide and it has a tummy-trouble sort of name – intracellular ·fermentation!

The next surprise is that when the grapes arrive from the vineyards, the whole bunch goes into the vat. Obviously, the weight of the grapes as the vat fills up starts another fermentation (the sort we're used to) by splitting the grapes and releasing their natural ferments. After a few days, the vat has a solid mass at the bottom, wine in the middle and grapes on top. This is the maceration period, still with carbon dioxide acting as a seal. The contents of this sealed vat, except the solid pomace at the bottom, is then pumped into another vat and completes its fermentation. Finally, the pomace is pressed and joins the newly made wine. The purpose of this extraordinary exercise is to make stable wine very quickly, of total grapey freshness and full colour. It is largely practised in Beaujolais and the Midi.

This explanation, in depth, of *macération carbonique* is really only an excuse to tell quite a charming story.

The scene is a small château in the Beaujolais – it is vintage time and the grapes are about to arrive. One member of our party usually buys a large chunk of the château's production, not from the owner, but via a *négociant*, who is with us.

Just before the first batch of grapes arrive, the owner himself arrives – perhaps that is protocol. The *négociant* introduces him to the buying member of our party. But the owner is aghast. How is it possible for his best English customer to appear, as it were, from the clouds of carbon dioxide and unannounced. The grapes are arriving and the priorities of the owner are stretched to the limit. He tries desperately to make the right noises to his customer, then suddenly just gives up and joins his cellarmen for carbonic action. No one likes to see a man literally in some distress, but when he makes totally the right decision, one admires the chap that much more.

7. False. This may sound a contradiction, but sherry in many ways is a contradiction. Yet it all starts so simply. The area of production lies between Jerez de la Frontera, Puerto de Santa Maria and Sanlucar de Barrameda, all in Andalucia in south west Spain. The Albariza soil is chalk (plus a heavier secondary soil – Barros), and if one drives out to one or two of the prime sherry vineyards within easy distance of Jerez, say Macharnudo or Carrascal, by the time the car gets back to the hotel it is white.

The grape is Palomino which is harvested in early September and today is pressed and fermented like any other dry white wine – completely; leaving no residual sugar. The days of stamping the grapes in studded boots are history, but not ancient history. Thus at its birth all sherry is dry – bone dry. It may later be coloured and indeed sweetened by the Pedro Ximénez (PX) or the Muscatel grape and both go through a special form of fermentation which admittedly involves the addition of brandy to stop complete fermentation and achieve maximum sweetness. The colouring wine which adjusts the colour of a brand of sherry, so it is always the same on reaching the public, is a boiled-up syrup of low alcohol.

Once the extremely violent fermentation dies down, the pale white wine begins to behave in a contradictory manner, showing a will of its own. The result is that no two casks of new wine from the same patch of vineyard necessarily develop the same traits. The best of them grow, on their surface, a creamy, cheesey, white yeast called '*flor*' and are encouraged so to do by keeping to a minimum the fortifying brandy. All sherry is fortified in stages, after the fermentation, so it eventually reaches the public with between 17 per cent and 19 per cent alcohol – give or take a little.

This '*flor*' is a culture that can be produced in the laboratory and is used by all countries who produce their own 'sherry'. In Jerez de la Frontera it produces itself naturally, as it also does in the Jura district of France where their *vin jaune* tastes like unfortified sherry.

Because of the contradictory behaviour of the wine, after fermentation is complete, literally each individual cask of the new wine has to be tasted (actually 'nosed') to decide the style of sherry it is likely to become and how best to help it on its way. This classification may take two years or more, before the *añada* (an unblended sherry of one harvest) is allotted a place with his brothers in the maturing system of the cellar (*bodega*).

We all know the Englishman is apt to talk too much about the weather and the Frenchman his liver. If the conversation wanes in Jerez, it can always be rekindled by querying the number of styles a sherry can become. The enthusiast can name around thirty.

At this early stage, the tasters are really looking for three basic types.

Fino: a wine that has produced '*flor*' and, if properly nursed, will become a light, fresh, dry wine, eventually fortified to little more than 17 per cent alcohol.

Oloroso: a wine that has failed to produce adequate '*flor*' and whose efforts have now been killed by the addition of alcohol. Fine *olorosos* can make rich, deep-tasting sherries; the Spanish races prefer them dry, the Anglo-Saxon not so dry. The very best *olorosos* can also produce Palo Cortado, today coming back into favour with a certain 'chic' cachet. You smell *oloroso*, you taste *oloroso*, then you suddenly think you are drinking *fino*. In effect, you're getting the best of both worlds.

Raya: a failed *oloroso*, if you like, fully competent of making a commercial, medium sherry and then often labelled *amontillado*.

8. Vermouth. The 'botanical' room of an Italian Vermouth set-up is fascinating; herbs from all over the world, in solid, liquid and powder form will be found there.

The question is: is Vermouth a wine? Well, 70 per cent of the contents of the bottle is 100 per cent vino – so it is obviously a flavoured wine.

9. False. Within the EEC countries, Chablis can only be a dry, white wine from a legally defined area of Burgundy, made from the Chardonnay grape, but in the USA California-made pink Chablis may still be found.

10. The answer is neither, as this is a simple catch question. Chaptalization/gallization is the addition of sugar to unfermented grape-juice (must) to ensure adequate alcohol after fermentation. To my knowledge sugar is never added to wine, but there is never a 'never' in wine matters. *Liqueur d'expedition*, a mixture of sugar, wine and possibly brandy, at various degrees of sweetness, is added to most champagnes, immediately prior to final corking.

Chaptalization is legal in France, covering all wine areas of red, white and rosé wines from Reims down to and including northern Rhône. It can be sanctioned in exceptionally bad vintages even further south, indeed in 1984 it was allowed as far south as, but excluding, Châteauneuf-du-Pape. It is legally controlled and limited, the yardstick being about 2 per cent additional alcohol, to the potential alcohol of unsugared musts.

In certain years, some of the great names in Bordeaux are forced to chaptalize or have no wine – 1977 must have been that way. It is extremely widespread at all levels in Burgundy, and perhaps criticized by the younger school of winemakers who do not accept that 'it is necessary to bring the wine into better balance ...'.

Gallization is almost automatic in Germany, particularly in the Mosel up to *Qualität* standard. The musts of eventual *Prädikat* wines may not be sugared.

To Spain, sugar is a sour word. Spain is not allowed to chaptalize and if their wines have insufficient alcohol (*vide* sherry), they must be fortified with Spanish brandy.

Incidentally, it should be noted that chaptalization is a forbidden practice in California.

11. True. If one pressed black grapes, however hard they were crushed, the best colour the juice would attain might be something between rose and tawny. The colour of the pulp of black and white grapes is usually the same. Think of the Beaujolais grape Gamay. Its official name is Gamay

Noir à Jus Blanc. It is so named not because it is unusual for a black grape to give off white juice, but because there is another Gamay which does give off reddish juice (which is very exceptional) – the Gamay Coloré.

Red wine achieves its colour by fermenting on the skins. The procedure is as follows:

The black grapes arrive at the *cuverie,* crush house, call it what you will – the cellar where the fermentation takes place. They then pass through a machine which takes off the stems and splits the grapes. The whole of the grape, less the stems and sometimes even they are included, is pumped into the fermenting vat and fermentation on the skins takes place. The very weight of the grapes produces juice and this juice takes from the skins tannin, colour and possibly aroma. The longer fermentation on the skins continues, the greater the intake of colour and tannins, both essential elements for a long maturing wine – a *'vin de garde'*.

There is one minor snag, as the amount of juice increases, the residue of skins, pips and whatever, helped by the natural carbon dioxide, keeps floating to the top of the vat and usually forms a mass or lump. The French call this mass the *'chapeau'*, the Spaniards the *'sombrero'* and English speakers call it the cap. There are endless ways of siphoning the juice (now almost wine) over the cap and indeed of breaking up the mass when it forms.

Simple methods are so often practical and one hot afternoon in Pommard, I watched a cellarman, totally nude and unconcerned, place a plank across the top of an open vat and dangle from it while his legs broke up the *chapeau.* Seeing him once more on terra firma, I had the impression of an ancient Briton, covered in woad. The cellar cat also strolled over and took a professional interest in the bouquet of his legs.

After a few days, or even weeks, the winemaker decides there has been enough intake of colour and tannins, and the juice is run off into maturing casks. The cap now falls to the bottom of the fermenting vat and changes its name to *marc* or pomace.

A pressing of this 'everything except juice' does now take place, in fact two or three pressings. The first pressing will be used by the winemaker. It will be matured separately but in the same way as the new wine, and when eventually the bottling period approaches, the winemaker will decide how much of this first pressing of the pomace should be added to his blend.

Making white wine is totally different, because no colour is required. The white grapes arrive at the *cuverie* and are pressed immediately, usually with stalks in Europe, usually without in North America. The juice and only the juice is pumped into the fermenting vat and *voilà*, no problems about '*chapeau*', '*sombrero*' or 'cap'.

12. (a) Hearty California Burgundy is the brain-child of Ernest and Julio Gallo of Modesto, California. The Gallo brothers, who are still totally involved, have in their own lifetime built up a vast wine Empire. For once, that trite phrase, 'They are a legend in their own lifetime', actually applies. Reputedly, their sales exceed a million cases a week. Size and quality have not always been closely linked in wine circles. The 'jug' and more recently the 'varietal' wines of E. and J. Gallo have proved this to be out-of-date thinking. Their California Burgundy tastes exactly as the name suggests – hearty – with the suggestion of a sweet farewell.

(b) Bernkasteler Doktor is one of the prime German vineyards of the middle Mosel. The grapes are 100 per cent Riesling (too obvious to mention on the label), the soil and notably the position are ideal. Rather curiously, one has always heard that extra heat favours the vineyard site, being generated by the sun reflected off the slate roofs of the 'film-set' town of Bernkastel. Dienhard and Co. Ltd. of Koblenz and London have long been a major owner. They have even produced a sparkling version.

(c) Tignanello is a vineyard owned by L. and P. Antinori who have traded from Florence for a mere 600 years. It is situated in the Chianti *classico* area, but is not a DOCG Chianti. Admittedly, it is vinified with a majority of the classical Chianti grape Sangiovese, but without any addition of white grapes and, instead, a healthy shot in the arm of Cabernet. These last two points cut across the rules of DOCG. Tignanello follows the Bordeaux style of ageing for two years in '*barriques*'. Tignanello is only one of Antinori's Bordeaux style wines and reflects the great

rarity of an ancient firm brimming over with modern ideas.
(d) Quinta de Vargellas, the word '*quinta*' can be translated as 'estate', is one of the finest port vineyards in the Douro. The property is owned by Taylor, Fladgate and Yeatman. In the great port years, when Taylors declare a vintage, all the wines from Vargellas are usually required to enhance the eventual blend. In the lesser years, when Taylors do not declare a vintage, they may well market only Quinta de Vargellas as a vintage port of a single *quinta*. This system is not peculiar to Taylors, nor is it universal. Any *quinta* may adopt it if it fits in with their particular marketing plans.
(e) Taltarni is a recent winery in Victoria, Australia with sights set high. It is closely associated with the California Clos du Val and each has a French winemaker whose father Monsieur Portet was '*régisseur*' at Château Lafite. Surely, this is a rarity!
(f) Gran Coronas Reserva, sometimes known as Gran Coronas Black Label, is the highest quality red wine of the astonishing Torres family – Manuel, the father, Miguel, the winemaker son and daughter Marimar the saleslady extraordinaire.

Torres have made the area of Vilafranca de Penedes, north of Barcelona, one of the most fascinating wine areas of Spain. Comparison with Rioja, where the DO requires only the use of the traditional Spanish grapes, is hardly applicable. Rioja is classic Spanish at its best. Penedes is experimental Spanish, equally at its best. One finds, planted in the area, the noble grapes of Spain plus a host of noble French grapes, both black and white.

Gran Coronas Reserva is the product of 90 per cent Cabernet Sauvignon and 10 per cent Cabernet Franc. Bulk ageing is in new oak casks followed by mighty ageing in bottle. It is a magnificent wine in its own right. It has also scored higher marks in blind tastings than many of the greatest Cabernets of the world – which is less important. The first rule of any blind tasting is that the order of tasting is such that no wine can obviously mask the true merits of another. With the best will in the world, this is almost impossible to arrange in an international tasting of red wines. White international tastings seem to work more accurately. International tastings of Chardonnays seem to

Château Palmer, home of the third growth Margaux, one of the greatest Bordeaux wines.

give a truer result than those of Cabernets.

(g) There are a number of Bordeaux châteaux which, by today's thinking, deserve a higher rating. Château d'Angludet of Margaux is possibly one. It is included in this question as the firm who owns it, Peter A. Sichel of Bordeaux, and whose principal lives there, also has a stake in Château Palmer, a third growth Margaux classified in 1855 which certainly many people feel fully deserves a higher classification.

(h) Laborie is the superb, yet simple, guest-house of the Ko-operatiewe Wignbouwers Vereniging (KWV), the governing body of South African wine and brandies. It is situated just outside Paarl.

It produces red and white still wines and a sparkling blanc de noirs under the Laborie label. It is also a centre for endless wine symposia and tastings.

13. In the Napa Valley of California, where the Christian Brothers make brandy by traditional pot-still as well as modern continuous still. Their XO is highly rated by tasters although it has the distinctive vanilla aroma which always distinguishes Californian brandy from French cognac or Armagnac.

14. After fermentation of red wine, its 'lees' (that is the skins, pips and everything left in the fermenting vat after the wine has been pumped into maturing barrels) is pressed two or three times. The first pressing of this *vin de presse* will be matured in the usual way as a small proportion is often used in the final blend to give added backbone. It also makes a *vin ordinaire* which may well be given to the grape-pickers.

Table Manners

1. Alsatian wines. The wines of Alsace are of course French Rhein wines.

2. Basically there are three:

   i. To separate from the wine any deposit there may be in the bottle.
   ii. To aerate the wine and allow it to breathe.
   iii. Aesthetic – some decanters add decoration to one's table.

The cynic might add a fourth answer that if you serve your guests wine from a decanter, you can possibly get away with murder. Oscar Wilde described cynicism as 'a young man's apology for knowledge' – so let's ignore this one.

   Getting rid of the deposit must be right, but it appears less and less as the clarification of wine becomes ever more sophisticated. It is rarely seen outside Europe, nor in wines from Greece, Italy, Portugal and Spain. It is, or should be, found in French wines which have been in bottle a few years, usually earlier in Bordeaux than Burgundy. At the moment we are only speaking of table wines. Curiously, the Burgundians are shy of decanting. They are chauvinistic to the core and may well feel that what is good for Cabernet Sauvignon must be bad for Pinot Noir. Occasionally, their guests suffer from this and if you happen to be served last you may have a glass of deposit. 'Simple peasants' though many claim to be, they still know more about PR with regard to wine than anyone in the business. Proof of this is that of all the wine societies in the world, only the *Confrérie des Chevaliers du Tastevin* is totally international. Similar remarks apply to the annual Hospices de Beaune sale. Their sense of PR was fully operative when seen on TV where a prominent Burgundian was seen solemnly decanting an old Burgundy by turning the handle of a 'decanting cradle' which gently and in one motion tilts the bottle towards the various glasses. They

The ultimate decanting cradle which can operate three sizes of bottle – half bottle, bottle and magnum.

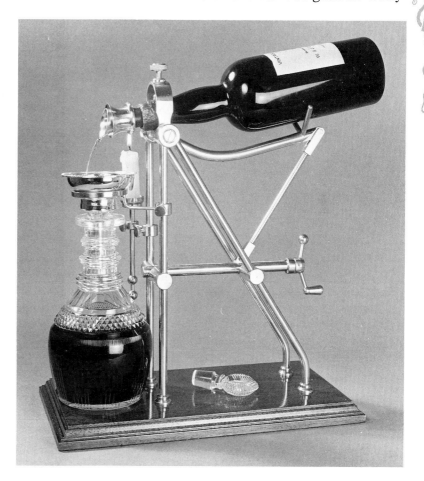

make wonderful wedding presents (when the mind goes blank) but I have never seen one in action, except for that one time on television!

May I suggest that if a bottle of Burgundy contains any deposit, it should be decanted like any other wine, and nothing does it better than the cradle job. I cannot recall ever having a conversation in California about decanting; nor, for that matter, early opening for 'breathing' purposes. The problem for the average European wine-man is that we are able to visit California rarely, and each visit we find some incredible new theory being put into practice which is always intriguing, and one forgets the old stand-bys.

Genuine vintage port is always decanted. One is speaking of Portuguese port of a single year which has spent two years in wood and is then bottled plus all the 'debris' which is usually fined, racked or filtered out of the wine – in order to mature in bottle. Such wines throw a heavy 'crust'.

There is no mystique in decanting, as long as one remembers it is not pouring the total bottle of wine into another container. Its first purpose is to get the wine into another container, leaving the deposit in the bottle. Stage 1 is stand the bottle upright for 12 to 24 hours, preferably in the room where it will be drunk. The deposit then falls to the bottom of the bottle. Now draw the cork with the bottle still upright. Next, place a light between the decanter and the bottle and slowly, repeat slowly, pour the wine, over the light, into the decanter. Soon you will notice a black stain rising up the bottle; when it reaches the neck, stop decanting. Maybe you will lose two inches or so of muddy wine, which is always useful in the kitchen. Traditionally the light is a candle, but should it be used, make sure the wine is out of range when you blow out the candle. More functional is a stand-up torch which allows you to bend the front part to face the ceiling.

The method above is easy and ideal when you have plenty of time. If you suddenly want to decant an old red wine, it has to be done from the horizontal. Carry the wine carefully from the bin in the horizontal position and place it into a wine basket. Steady the basket and bottle against a solid background and remove the cork. Pick up both the

A splendid Victorian wine funnel, ideal for port decanting.

basket and the bottle as one entity and decant over a light as before.

Vintage port is decanted in exactly the same way as table wine. If you have to do it without previous warning, there is no problem. The crust is so heavy that you can decant via muslin from any position. Finger the muslin into the decanter and pour. Muslin will not stop table wine deposit, which is too fine. So ends the first reason for decanting.

The second reason is to allow the wine to breathe, a much debated hypothesis. Some modern wine oenologists say that letting the wine breathe is all nonsense. Oxidation is bad for any wine, they claim. The traditionalist, and I suggest the average château owner, allows his wine to breathe for an hour or two before consumption, and can prove he is right by taste – or can he? We have all had a fine wine served at a meal which suddenly 'opens up' and improves, or if very old dies in the glass. The former suggests the wine has not been open long enough, the latter that the wine should have been decanted straight into the guests' glasses. That is all a little bit too simple because various experiments have taken place tasting the same wine 'blind', each sample of which has been opened at a different time, and always the results come out pretty well inconclusive. I have a feeling that once a wine reaches a certain state of maturity (we are speaking of fine wine), it acts totally as an individual. Some wines out of the same case act or react differently.

One example proves nothing, but very briefly the following is a true story. I dined with a very up-to-the-minute wine agent in Vancouver. On the sideboard stood a bottle of Château Lynch Bages 1961 which I eyed longingly. As the meat course appeared, so the bottle was opened and decanted straight into our glasses. The result was utterly delicious (frankly, so perfect, it made me feel old and out of date). A few months' later, but in England, there was a chance of repeating the exercise with the identical wine. Total disaster. The wine was tight shut till the last few sips. In Canada no aeration worked, in England with exactly the same wine no aeration was a total failure – why?

Another true story, which might interest or possibly be derided by the Californians. A notable French wine merchant was dining at my home. It would have been stupid to have served him even the best French wine from my cellar. In the event, we had a New Zealand Chardonnay and an extremely good Cabernet Sauvignon from Napa. We never play games at home, and I was about to tell him the wines when he asked if he might guess them. There was no way he could guess the Chardonnay, but he really should have spotted the red as Californian – and he knew it, but failed to. His explanation was interesting. He said, 'I should have got the Californian, but you see it's the first time I've had a top Californian properly served. You must have opened that wine at least two hours ago and of course it's decanted. Normally they are served to me straight from the bottle.' I suggested the phrase 'properly served' certainly applied to European wines, but not necessarily Californian. Frankly, I do not know the answer, but am fairly convinced there is no set answer as to how long one should allow a quality red table wine to breathe (even if at all) before consumption. But the public want that information. At my home it is usually two hours for red table wine, probably one hour for white wine and maybe twelve hours for vintage port. But for anyone who is still blessed with any of the great pre-war vintages either Bordeaux or Burgundy, these may well have to be opened and poured straight into the glasses and indeed have been known to die in the glass as one is drinking.

The third reason to decant, which is purely aesthetic, needs a word of warning. Unless the neck of the decanter is wide enough, pouring into it from the bottle can be troublesome.

3. In practice, it must increase the chance of the sediment being poured into the glass. Each time the *sommelier* pours, the tilting up and down of the cradled bottle mixes the wine and the sediment. Even so, the use of a wine basket is an attractive way of serving red wine and the average reds have no deposit. We live in an age when presentation and packaging is all-important and the wine basket doubtless plays its part. One would hope that the *sommelier* had been briefed as to which wines on the list are better decanted and advises the customer accordingly.

It is also common practice for the *sommelier* to smell the

cork of any bottle he opens. This gives the customer confidence and, using the presentation argument, should continue. But in your own home beware, rather curiously, a cork with a foreign smell may have no effect on the wine at all. Conversely, although the cork smells clean, the wine may still be 'corked'.

Some people pretaste a wine, almost expecting to find a fault which is very apt to create one. Today, an out-of-condition wine, no matter what the reason, is a rarity.

Obviously, it occasionally happens and, if in a restaurant, one's sympathies are with the host. He pretastes the wine and passes it – in three or four minutes' time, it is obviously 'corked'. Conversely, a wine with a doubtful smell-taste, after a little aeration and by the time the *sommelier* has been summoned, has righted itself.

There is an old, old wine story (source unknown) of a *sommelier* who possibly took his calling too seriously. On this occasion, he serves the lady on the right of the host before the latter has had a chance to sample the wine. The host discreetly makes signs for the wine to be poured into his own glass. The *sommelier* after a hiccup or two, announces 'In this restaurant, ladies are always served first.' The host concedes that this shows a certain chivalry, but tries to explain he merely wanted to taste the wine in case it was 'corked'. Another hiccup or two and the *sommelier* indignantly states 'In this restaurant all our wines are corked.'

4. The answer reputedly given by André Simon, and one must of course remember all great men are so often quoted as the 'true' source of any story, was as follows:
   'You cannot drink any wine with grapes, that would be incest.'

5. By and large he would have been right. But there are always exceptions. In the summer and speaking of red wines which, by their nature, are normally drunk young, such wines are definitely improved by serving from an ice bucket, not by keeping in the fridge for twelve hours.

It is common practice in southern Rhône (not a happy hunting ground for white wines) to serve the current vintage red Côtes du Rhône chilled, and with dishes normally associated with white wines.

It is normal sense (although often done for chic reasons) to serve, in summer-time, the current year's Beaujolais, Chianti, Provence and Midi reds from an ice bucket.

Now to red wines of above-basic quality. Do nothing to chill them and equally nothing to warm them, no matter what the time of year. If to your taste the red wine appears too cold, warm the bowl of the glass in your palm. If it appears too hot, allow your palate and the wine to acclimatize to each other – they will.

White wines are more difficult. It is a totally personal thing how cold one likes one's dry white wines (sweet wines can absorb appreciably more chilling), but try and avoid too cold a wine and you'll enjoy it more. A really high quality white wine needs very little chilling. Finally, when the *sommelier* turns up with your white wine correctly in an ice bucket, it often pays, after the first glass, to put the bottle on the table and forget about the ice bucket. Don't be shy about it.

6. It is not a question of 'getting away' with an Italian wine, it is the obvious answer – you must serve it. The wines of no country go better with their national dishes than the wines of Italy. No matter what your expense account position may be, Chianti with Cannelloni and Valpolicella with Vitello beat any classed growth from the Médoc.

Tasting and testing fine German wines.

7. Muscadet de Sèvre et Maine.

8. Yes. The Riesling is the prime white grape of the Rheingau – no problem. But around the village of Assmannshausen are vineyards planted with the Spätburgunder, the German Pinot Noir, which produces a pale red wine. The wine is thoroughly enjoyed by many and therefore achieves one of the essential requirements of any wine. One might think that after a full day's tasting of Rhein wines (the most tiring of all still wine tastings) one would rush for a glass of Spätburgunder, but this is not so. The average taster, including the locals, downs a glass of cold beer. Similarly, after a heavy French tasting, there is something very cleansing about a long Scotch and soda.

9. The definite mistakes are:

i. The sparkling rosé could not have been Vouvray whose sparkling wines are only white.
ii. *Manzanilla* is only matured at Sanlucar de Barrameda.
iii. Château Petrus contains no Cabernet Sauvignon.
iv. Château Mouton Rothschild was not a *premier grand cru* till 1973.

In more detail, at a 'classy' dinner, if the aperitif is a sparkling wine wrapped in a napkin, one automatically thinks of champagne, which makes tasting almost impossible. Anyway, tasting sparkling wines blind is probably the most difficult tasting. Scrutiny of the bubbles is often helpful. Not only should they be tiny but they should form almost a mist rather than be seen as individual bubbles. This normally proves slow cold fermentation. Vino's wine may have been 'Crémant de Loire'.

Manzanilla sherry is an oddity. It is 'made' only in the open *bodegas* of the small port of Sanlucar de Barrameda (lunch distance from Jerez and essential for the true appreciation of *langostina*) where the salt sea air gives it a distinct and, to most people, delightful aromatic flavour. It is a *fino* and is matured under a white covering of the bacteria *flor*. But move it up the road to Jerez and it becomes more like a straightforward *fino*. Equally a Jerez *fino* catches some of the *manzanilla* traits if moved to Sanlucar. It is the one wine that cannot travel (even locally) without forfeiting something of its birthright.

Vino's description, white Vougeot, is just OK. The full AC Clos de Vougeot is red only but the small amount of *premier cru* white wine it produces is strictly speaking called Clos Blanc de Vougeot.

High quality sweet Graves are still to be found in the southern area of Graves. Semillon grapes take first place plus possibly a little Muscadelle. Indeed their reputation certainly dates back to earlier than the fine red wines for which the Graves area is now best known.

My sympathy is rather with Vino over his finding of a Cabernet Sauvignon bouquet in Petrus. Perhaps Petrus is too extreme an example as its make-up is usually only 5 per cent Cabernet Franc – the rest is Merlot. But I have tasted other Pomerols with a higher percentage of Cabernet Franc and confidently proclaimed Cabernet Sauvignon. Château Mouton Rothschild achieved *premier grand cru* status in 1973 (the top strip of label by Picasso) – the only château ever to achieve promotion since the original classification of 1855.

The French dining club showed great professionalism in serving an unadorned peach with the Gewürztraminer *vendange tardive*. So often really superb dessert wines are ruined by some ghastly gooey sweet covered in chocolate and cream.

10. Because you, I and most others have more than once mistaken the red wine in the decanter for Burgundy when it was Bordeaux or vice versa, and no doubt will on occasion continue so to do. And for no rational reason.

Bordeaux has a maritime climate. Burgundy, 400 long miles away, is the centre of a land mass and nowhere near the sea. As it happens, the autoroute makes it near Paris. Today, Beaune is luncheon distance from Paris and we are told is now the main attraction for visitors to France after Versailles.

Almost all Burgundies, red and white, are one-grape wines; in Bordeaux, one-grape wines are the exception.

Many people find red Burgundy, particularly if young, almost sweet compared to Bordeaux. Analytically, this is not so, but certainly red Burgundy in youth can be softer, rounder and easier to get on with than Bordeaux. Some of us find old Bordeaux have a sweet suggestion. Dining with the proprietor of a prestigious château, his 1929 was very kindly served. In impeccable schoolboy French, I happened to say, 'You know, Monsieur, this wine is almost sweet'. After we had picked Monsieur X off the floor and dusted him down, it was explained that the fault was not with the wine but with my French. Even so, the Frenchmen there, who agreed about the sweetness, didn't seem to know the right word to use – it is not '*moelleux*' incidentally.

All this about Burgundy being a one-grape wine – does it really matter? Probably not, but it could make it less complex with age. However, from Chablis to the bottom of Beaujolais, all the white wines are Chardonnay (it is easier to forget about Pinot) except one, made from the lesser grape Aligote. From the Côte d'Or, all red wine is made with the Pinot Noir, until the Mâconnais where the Gamay Noir à Jus Blanc begins to take over. Throughout Beaujolais, the Gamay reigns. The Gamay and the Pinot Noir get together as grapes when vinifying Bourgogne Passe-Tout-Grains. Bordeaux's greatest strength is her château bottled wines, Burgundy's good fortune is to have Beaujolais next door.

The Bordeaux château entity of grapes grown and fermented, and of the wines aged and bottled within the same enclave, gives an authenticity that is hard to match.

A château bottled Bordeaux is the same from whoever it is bought. A Burgundy generic or vineyard *appellation* of the same vintage will vary according to the *négociant-éleveur* who matured and bottled the wine. His name on the label is all-important. You will notice, on a correct wine list, château bottled wines show no supplier – only the classification and the area from which the wine comes. Yet each Burgundy shows the supplier–bottler; his name guarantees his particular style.

Bordeaux, château bottled or otherwise, is not normally a one-grape wine. Speaking of the main red wine areas Médoc/Graves, the grapes in use are the Cabernet Sauvignon, the Cabernet Franc, tempered by Merlot and perhaps Petit Verdot – the château owner decides in which proportions but it is rare for the Cabernet Sauvignon not to be the major grape. Not so across the Dordogne into St Emilion and Pomerol where the soil prefers the Merlot, with the Cabernet Franc and/or Sauvignon as second grapes.

The major grape of the dry white Bordeaux is the Sauvignon, best softened with Semillon and even Muscadelle. The sweet wines do it the other way round, Semillon takes pride of place, with Sauvignon and Muscadelle second and third.

From Bordeaux, back to the Burgundy region – to the Beaujolais. Beaujolais is a funny one whether unadorned, Supérieures or Villages, it is still Beaujolais – nothing more. It is not Burgundy. Yet its northern half has nine regions known as the *cru* (growth) Beaujolais which can call themselves Burgundy, but never do, since each of the

55

wines has its own *appellation contrôlée*. But why only *cru* when no *cru* in the Côte d'Or would settle for less than *premier* or even *grand*. For the very few who do not know them by heart, here are the nine Beaujolais regions. The first four may well be in that position in certain vintages: Fleurie; Moulin-à-Vent; Juliénas; Brouilly; Chénas; Chiroubles; Côte de Brouilly; Morgon; and St Amour. One can now no longer escape comparing the two great wines Bordeaux and Burgundy – it has to be very simple, but the difference is there, as few people like both equally.

Perhaps Bordeaux is too tannic to be drunk young, yet in certain vintages, notably 1982, the very *petits* châteaux were/are delicious at a very early age. Burgundy is always good at an early age, if it is a good Burgundy, and you don't have to wait so long to enjoy its *grand crus*. But for Bordeaux, the great châteaux are worth waiting for.

11. Château Lafitte – Premières Côtes de Bordeaux. This is just one of many 'Lafites' and 'Latours' destined to confuse the Bordeaux wine novice.

12. The obvious answer is both but that is difficult.

The two main essentials of a wine glass are to show the colour of the wine clearly, and to be of a size so that the wine can safely be rotated. This swirling of the wine in the glass brings out the bouquet – aroma – smell.

No one wants the colour of the wine exaggerated, which may happen if the stem of the glass is coloured or the glass is partially cut-glass. You should therefore have a totally plain glass which by its nature is hardly decorative. As to its size, you should choose a glass with a slightly tulip-shaped bowl and a capacity of a comfortable 200 millilitres. If filled to about half, the wine can easily be rotated. Such a glass is totally suitable for red, white or rosé wines, still or sparkling. The stem should be long enough to hold the glass without touching the bowl – essential for white wines. Exactly the same shaped, plain glass but in a smaller size is suitable for fortified wines.

13. Sherry is the wine on offer and the skilled server is called a *venenciador* – note the fistful of glasses he fills as one from his *venencia*.

SECTION
II

A Miscellany

Vignette

1. What do the following initials (all connected with wine) stand for: QmP, DOCG, LBV, VDN.

2. We have to thank the Church and, indeed, individual clerics for their dedicated nurturing of wines, as of all the humanities. Originally, perhaps various abbeys had to tend vines for sacramental reasons, but fortunately they soon cottoned on to the joys of gracious living, much to the benefit of us all.

Can you place the following?

    (a) Kir
    (b) Abbaye of Hautvillers
    (c) Abbaye of Citeaux
    (d) Kloster Eberbach

3. Ireland has no snakes (possibly thanks to St Patrick). What is not found in Chile?

4. Charles the Great, King of the Franks and Emperor of the Romans who ruled and warred during the first century AD, gave his name to two Burgundy *appellations*. Which are they?

5. Between the years 1969 and 1978 inclusive, there was one vintage when red Bordeaux achieved far higher quality than red Burgundy, and another vintage when exactly the reverse happened. Can you name the two vintages concerned?

6. It is often a thought-teaser as to whether a wine name in Italy is that of a grape or place. How about Montepulciano – grape or geography?

7. The wines of Europe are constantly seeking to gain a higher *appellation* than the one they have. The VDQS wines of France reach for the AOC. The DOC wines of Italy strive for their G. The vintners of Pomerol are totally unimpressed – why?

8. 'Here, *mon cher*,' said the *vigneron*, slightly swaying from one sabot on to the other, 'our finest areas bear the name of one of your favourite wines'. 'Yes,' I replied, 'and the grapes planted there, have the name of another'. Where were the two of us chatting?

9. Way back around AD 400 a renowned Roman poet lived (was even born?) in Bordeaux. St Emilion honours him to this day but posterity remembers best his poem of homage to the Mosel. Can you give his name?

10. (a) The fame of the 1983 Burgundy vintage (comparable to 1964) may now have been slightly dented by 1985 whose white wines appear on an equal standing to their reds.
   (b) 1984 was not Germany's greatest vintage, but thanks to the noble Riesling, a number of QmP wines were made in the Mosel area.
   (c) The vignerons of Sauternes have to vintage late, when a change in the weather could wreck everything. Even so, they made great wines in 1976 and 1983.
   (d) 'I have made a better wine than I have ever made before,' spoken of the 1984 Muscadet by a leading producer.
Which of the above statements could prove right? Which must be wrong?

11. What is the wine connection between Dior, Cartier and Montecarlo?

12. Dionysius, son of Zeus and Semele, the latter the daughter of Cadmus of Thebes, is better known as whom?

13. Can you complete the following couplet?

'If all be true that I do think
There are five reasons we should drink ...'

14. A holy trio connected with winemaking – but whereabouts? Saints Barbara, Maria and Ynez are the clues.

15. Who was Virginia Dare and what is her connection with the world of wine?

16. These wines may have you foxed in more ways than one. Can you explain?

17. The barrels on the floor are encircled with willow hoops. Does this suggest to you that the cellar is in Bordeaux or Burgundy?

Answers on page 68

II

Tips of the (Wine) Trade

1. Very occasionally Grandpa turns up with a dust-covered bottle of cognac and the knowledge that it has been in the family cellar since well before World War I. The bottle bears no vintage but the word cognac is just discernible. What value would one put on such cognac?

2. Who wants Liebfraumilch? Around 60 per cent of German wine exports are Liebfraumilch, so quite a few people do. Within Germany, Mosel would love an equivalent of a Liebfraumilch. What is their latest bid?

3. Which two drinks are affectionately known as:
   (a) The widow   (b) Sticky green

4. Which of these alcoholic drinks, if any, must be bottled in their area of production?
   (a) Portuguese vintage ports (d) Alsatian wines
   (b) Spanish cream sherry   (e) QmP German wines
   (c) Cognac   (f) Most whiskies

5. Name the year in which the latest classification of Bordeaux wines – a pretty middle-class effort – took place.

6. The *Harmsworth Encyclopedia* early this century has an interesting article on Bordeaux. There are 25 lines of typical Encyclopedia stuff, before one reads 'The wines of Bordeaux, famed since the 4th century are of the first importance . . .' Prior to that, one learns that Transatlantic steamers stop at Pauillac and that Bordeaux is the HQ of the 18th Army Corps! Eventually, one comes to 'Chief Exports' and once more one is on home ground, because the answer is 'Wines' – 15 242 789 imperial (18 305 675 US) gallons were exported in 1903. Can you guess the 'Chief Imports'?

7. A blend of wood ports bears no age on the label, nor do any sherries. That doesn't sound right, or is it?

8. The North Americans use the phrase 'buying futures', elsewhere the French words '*en primeur*' seem more in use. What is it all adding up to?

9. The introduction of new German wine laws in 1971 limited all German wine to three main categories. Can you name them?

10. The greatest Bordeaux wines are château bottled. Say château X produced, in one year, 1260 Bordeaux *barriques* of wine. When the time of bottling arrives, are all these barrels first blended together, or is each barrel bottled individually to maintain its particular characteristics?

11. At the worlds' wine auctions (ignoring ancient bottles of a historical interest), the first growth clarets plus Château Petrus invariably fetch a higher price than any *grand cru* red Burgundy. True or false?

12. What does the date shown on a bottle of wine signify (allowing for local rules which permit a percentage of other years to be used):
    (a) The year the wine was bottled?
    (b) The year in which the majority of grapes making the wine were harvested?

13. A bottle of wine sold in the EEC normally contains either 70 or 75 centilitres (cl for short). But what does the 'e' printed beside 70 cl (see photograph) signify?

14. Will a wine bottled in any recognised wine area taste the same when exported to another country (assuming that the wine has been correctly handled throughout the journey)?

Answers on page 74

What's in a Name

1. What message have the following words for you? One of them is not a wine, not a grape, not a vineyard and anti all three.

    (a) Vaucrains   (c) Volstead

    (b) Vaucluse   (d) Valais

2. What common denominator have the following?

    (a) Cucugnan   (c) Bessan

    (b) Uzege   (d) Allobrogie

3. All these 'Gs' are closely associated with wine, arguably in rising order of merit, but that depends on one's nationality and personal taste. Can you fully elucidate?

    (a) Grinzing   (c) Grèves

    (b) Grumello   (d) Grenouilles

4. There are a number of vineyards in France named *domaine* or *clos* 'so and so', but the *domaines* greatly outnumber the *clos* vineyards.

Clos 'so and so' is handicapped by the vineyard (as the word suggests) having to be within an enclosure. No such strings are attached to a *domaine*. Any vineyard may carry a *domaine* name as chosen by the owner. This somewhat cavalier use of the description *domaine* throughout France in no way detracts from the importance of the words '*domaine* bottled' which means the owner has raised and bottled the wine from his own vineyard.

Rather curiously, there is no AOC which includes the word *domaine*.

There are, however, five *clos* red Burgundies each covered by its own AOC. Can you name them?

5. Pouilly is an AC Burgundy, an AC Loire or an AC wine in both Burgundy and the Loire areas. Which?

6. Where might you find a port made in Madera?

7. Whatever is Edelzwicker? It sounds more like a Teutonic oath than a wine.

8. What is understood by the two French words:
  (a) *Floraison*   (b) *Veraison*

9. The following words crop up now and again in connection with wine. Can you give each a meaning?
  (a) Ullage   (c) *Venencia*
  (b) Cadet   (d) *Les Trois Glorieuses*

10. All German wines labelled *trocken* are very dry. Yet all German wines labelled *Trockenbeerenauslese* are sweet and luscious. This is not really as strange as it seems. Can you explain why please?

11. *Tastevinage* – obviously something to do with wine. Any ideas as to what?

12. How does one differentiate between the following. The first three phrases may be found on wines from any area in France. The last might apply to any German wine:
  (a) *Mis en bouteilles au château*
  (b) *Mis en bouteilles au domaine*
  (c) *Mis en bouteilles à la propriété*
  (d) *Erzeugerabfullung*

13. Left is a typical German label, in that it has the vintage (1985), the grape variety (Riesling), the region (Mosel), the classification (*Deutscher Tafelwein*) but also, rather mysteriously, a more prominent description, *Landwein der Saar*. What is *Landwein*?

The Fizz Quiz

1. This wine is designed to delight, never to deceive. Yet it was granted the *Appellation d'Origine Contrôlée* at the earliest possible moment, but does not show the fact on the label. Perhaps it is inverted snobbery. Have you guessed the wine?

2. Surely no village in the wine world is so aptly named to describe an excess of what it produces. The clue is the Montagne de Reims.

3. Formerly *blanc de blancs* primarily referred to champagne made only from white grapes. Today it is far more widely used. Can you name any AOC still white wine not made totally with white grapes?

4. Many sparkling wines in Catalonia are made by the *méthode champenoise* (a phrase which is still legal – but for how long?). The Spanish prefer the word '*cava*'. Which of the following points applicable to champagne are equally applicable to the *cava* wines of Spain:
- (a) The dead yeast cells, etc. are shaken on to the base of the first closure, which is a process known internationally by the French name *remuage*.
- (b) The normal blend is made up of approximately 60 per cent wine from black grapes and 40 per cent from white.
- (c) The quality of the wine produced is to a great extent thanks to the chalky soil.

5. This wine seems to age better standing on its head. Which wine is it?

6. Which, if any, of the following wines are made by a second fermentation in bottle and which is the odd man out?

| (a) Crémant d'Alsace | (c) Crémant de Bourgogne |
| (b) Crémant de Loire | (d) Crémant de Cramant |

7. Sekt and German bubbles are intimately related. Can you take it on from there and explain the various forms of Sekt available?

8. Surely the merchants of Champagne would have thought the American poet, Longfellow, guilty of abusing 'poetic licence' when he thanked his friend, Nicolas Longworth, for a case of wine with the following jingle:

> 'Very good in its way
> Is the Verzenay
> Or the Sillery, soft and creamy
> But ... wine
> Has a taste more divine
> More dulcit, delicious and dreamy.'

Which wine was the subject of the poem?

9. If somebody mentioned to you *'brut nature'* or *'brut integral'*, what would they probably be talking about?

10. The majority of Italian white wines are dry. Certain *appellations* produce either dry or sweet varieties. In the case where the wine is not dry, either the *abboccato* or *amabile* description appears on the label. To an Italian both words probably denote sweetness; to the less initiated the translation is more accurately (or usually) 'not so dry'. But one wine from Piedmont is sweet and it is sparkling. Can you name it?

11. Where is Chandon divorced from Moët?

12. A twist of the wrist and the fizz is poured but there is also another secret of pouring all sparkling wines. A good champagne server holds the bottle by the indentation in the glass of the base ('the punt') using his thumb, while the bottle rests on his four fingers. Why should this be?

66

Answers on page 95

I

Vignette

1. QmP – *Qualitätswein mit Prädikat* – covers the group of German wines whose original sugar reading (*Oechsle* scale) allows them to use one of the five *Prädikats* of quality permitted by the German wine laws of 1971.

DOCG – *Denominazione di Origine Controllata e Garantita* – is a recent addition to the DOC laws of Italy. It is reserved for exceptional wines and at the moment has only been awarded to five. They are Barbaresco and Barolo from Piedmont, and Brunello di Montalcino, Vino Nobile Di Montepulciano and Chianti (in 1984) from Tuscany. The DOCG wines carry a government seal of guarantee which is only granted after the wines have been tasted by an approved tasting panel. One can argue that Chianti is too large an area to produce a totality of high-quality wines. One can equally argue that the real danger of being turned down by the tasting panel will encourage today's lesser areas to try and improve their quality.

LBV – Late Bottled Vintage – as the name suggests, is a vintage port (of one harvest) bottled after a longer period in cask than the traditional vintage port. The latter spends two years in cask and the rest of its life in bottle, throwing a very heavy deposit. Late Bottled Vintage spends at least double that time in cask where it sheds much of its sediment. LBV is therefore lighter in colour and texture and throws less deposit. In practice, many shippers today prefer to bottle their LBV ports clear of all sediment.

VDN – *Vin Doux Naturel* – in various areas of the Midi of France, they make a sweet, fortified wine from the Muscat or similar grape. An example is the AC Muscat de Beaumes de Venise, an extremely attractive dessert wine from the Vaucluse.

2. (a) The Burgundians' most popular aperitif before World War II was known as *vin blanc cassis*. Traditionally, the recipe is Bourgogne Aligoté flavoured with cassis, a liqueur of blackcurrants. Since the war, the Burgundians, who have a flair for such things, have rechristened their very own aperitif Kir after an extremely gallant cleric and resistance leader Felix Kir. Today, Kir is totally inter-

A statue of Dom Pérignon in the forecourt of the Maison Moët et Chandon.

national and can be made of any dry white wine.

(b) The Abbaye Hautvillers was the spiritual home of Dom Pérignon where he was head cellarman in the early eighteenth century. Apparently his position was even senior to the Abbot, which is a nice thought, but unlikely. Hautvillers is adjacent to Epernay in Champagne. Among Dom Pérignon's many contributions to the emergence of champagne was his appreciation that a wine fermenting in bottle obviously needed a much stronger bottle and stopper. He also realized the benefits of blending wines from various grapes and vineyards, now known as the *cuvée*. In his old age, and blind, it was claimed he would blend his *cuvées* by tasting grapes rather than wines. A trick very few of us could emulate.

(c) From as early as the twelfth century until the French Revolution, vineyards in Burgundy (and in other parts of Europe) were cultivated and cared for by the monks of Citeaux. Today's vineyards of Clos Vougeot were at one time the property of the Cistercian order and their monks originally built the wall which encloses those vineyards. The buildings which now house the *Confrérie des Chevaliers du Tastevin* were originally built as the Abbey of Citeaux.

(d) During the same period that the Burgundian Cistercians were tending their vines, their German brothers were producing wines from the Steinberg, today a state *domaine*. Their abbey was Kloster Eberbach in the Rheingau, now a promotional centre of German wines.

3. *Phylloxera.* Their *Vitis vinifera* vines are not grafted to resistant root stocks and their wines (red primarily) from Bordeaux grape varieties can be excellent.

4. Charles the Great was, of course, Charlemagne. Reputedly he owned extensive vineyards in what is now Aloxe-Corton. His name is commemorated by two outstanding white Burgundies: Charlemagne and Corton Charlemagne. The names are interchangeable but frankly I cannot recall ever seeing a wine labelled just Charlemagne.

As far as wine is concerned the first century AD is fairly recent, bearing in mind grapes flourished in the Mediterranean before *Homo sapiens* walked the earth!

Historians enjoy the erudite exercise of tracing the origin of wine via Dionysius, the Etruscans, the Greeks, the Romans, even Mount Ararat.

5. 1969, in general terms, produced red Burgundies of high class and probably white Burgundies of the highest class. Again, in general terms, 1969 red Bordeaux is considered not among the great vintages.

1975 is the reverse, red Burgundy was a bit of a disaster but curiously its extremities, Chablis and Beaujolais, fared better. It was and still is considered a very good year in Bordeaux, but now with a question mark as to when the fruit will break through the tannin.

6. This time one cannot be totally wrong as it is both. In Tuscany, it is an ancient town whose vineyards produce one of the five DOCG wines – the red Vino Nobile Di Montepulciano.

In the hills of Abruzzi, it is a grape, making the deep red wine, Montepulciano d'Abruzzo.

7. Rather curiously, the châteaux of Pomerol have never officially been classified. There are plenty of unofficial classifications, but official or unofficial, nothing will knock Château Petrus off its unique pedestal.

8. In the Cognac area – the department of Charente in south-west France. On a map, the legally defined areas where grapes may be grown for distillation into cognac brandy look rather like a target. The centre spread of vineyards from whose wine the finest cognacs normally result, is the 'bull's eye' and known as Grande Champagne. The latter does not relate to the well-known wine but may come from the Latin word *campania* meaning 'open country'. One step down the scale is Petite Champagne which might be called an 'inner', and the 'outers' are made up of the vineyards of the Borderies, Fins Bois, Bon Bois and finally Bois Ordinaires.

A well-known brand of cognac might be a distillation of wines from the Grande and Petite Champagne plus wines from the Borderies and possibly Fins Bois.

Cognac is planted primarily with the white St Emilion

Taking a tasting sample from a barrel of cognac.

grape, a variety of Ugni Blanc; other white grapes are allowed but no black grapes. Thus, one has the apparent oddity of two vineyards bearing the great wine name champagne planted with grapes with the name of Bordeaux's famous St Emilion region.

It so happens that the wine champagne and cognac share two pretty vital similarities; they are chalk and blending. Chalk is equally important to the soils of both areas. In Cognac it is rich in the vineyards of Grande and Petite Champagne and less so as the area spreads out to the Bois Ordinaires.

The art of blending is essential to a champagne *cuvée* as indeed it is to a cognac brandy.

The whole basis of cognac is a balanced blend of all ages. Today, no major cognac house markets a vintage cognac distilled from the grapes of one year. Such cognacs, going back to the beginning of the century, maybe further, exist in Cognac. They are stored in small oak wood or when their wood ageing has been sufficient, in large glass 'Bonbonnes', but they are not sold commercially. They are used in small quantities, to enhance the merchants' standard blends.

Most cognacs are marketed with the name of the firm concerned plus an indication of quality. The initial quality is traditionally three star, but today, this seems to have given way to VS (very special) which leads one on to VSOP (very special old pale) and up to a variety of higher descriptions, notably Napoleon. These brandies (cognac is a brandy but certainly not all brandies are cognacs) are blends of various years. Even so, France requires the youngest spirit in the blend to be four years old, if it is labelled VSOP. Most countries have their own minimum age requirements for spirits. In the UK, all brandies must have spent three years in wood prior to release, while California brandy must be aged for two years in the barrel although it is normally aged for four years.

Cognacs may be labelled with the vineyard name – Grande Champagne or Grande Fine Champagne, the phrases are interchangeable. Sometimes one sees Fins Bois on the label. It is probably fair to say that most cognacs of a quality higher than VSOP are either from the Grande Champagne or a blend of Grande and Petite Champagne.

9. Ausonius: St Emilion claims that Château Ausone, which today enjoys their highest *appellation* shared only with Château Cheval Blanc, was surely built on the site of Ausonius' home. The Mosel, where he moved as tutor to the son of a Roman ruler (later returning to Bordeaux), claims his poem in praise of the beauties of the Mosel was never matched by anything he composed in France.

10. (a) Correct: Burgundy was blessed with two great vintages, 1983 and 1985. At this stage 1985 is probably leading by half a length. Certainly, the 1985 whites are clearly in front of their 1983 cousins. They are a firmer, more typical white Burgundy. The 1983s may be easier to drink, but they are soft and buttery.
(b) Totally incorrect: there were very few QmP wines made in the Mosel in 1984.
(c) Absolutely correct: but when the moment of drinking arrives, probably the 1983 will gain the higher marks.
(d) Spoken by the Marquis De Goulaine of his own Muscadet. Might equally well have been said by his neighbours.

11. Dior is part of the international company Moët and Chandon Champagne plus Hennessy Cognac. Cartier was the inventor of the hydrometer to determine alcohol in liquids.

Perhaps Madame Cartier, of jewellery fame, could once claim a drink association – years ago we were served Kirsch reputedly distilled from a cherry orchard of Madame Cartier. Our host also volunteered the information that Madame had joined the French association of '*Distillateurs*' so that her name would appear as the only '*Distallatrice*'. In the unlikely event of the story being accurate, a charming streak of individuality is apparent.

Montecarlo is Italian and Tuscan. It is indeed a DOC white wine much sought after in the environs of Lucca.

12. Bacchus the Greek and Roman God of wine.

13. The full couplet reads:

> '*If all be true that I do think
> There are five reasons we should drink
> Good wine, a friend or being dry
> Or lest we should be bye and bye
> Or any other reason why.*'

Henry Aldrich (1647–1710) from the Latin *Causae Bibendi* by John Sirmond (1589–1649).

14. The three holy ladies are to be found in California, south of the famed San Francisco Bay Area and north of Los Angeles. This section of the coast has an agreeably mild climate ideal for grape-growing and within the county of Santa Barbara the plantings are concentrated in the Santa Ynez Valley and the Santa Maria area. The most notable producer in terms of both quality and quantity is Firestone, co-owned by the tyre company and by Suntory of Japan. As a general rule white wines seem more successful here, particularly Chardonnay, Gewürztraminer and Johannisberg Riesling, but Pinot Noir is yielding some interesting cool-climate red wines.

15. Virginia Dare was the first child born of British parents in America and the name of a wine made from Scuppernong grapes (a variety of Muscadine from the species *Vitis rotundifolia* native to America). The wine and the name were popularized by 'Captain' Paul Garrett, born during the Civil War and by 1903 the owner of five wineries in North Carolina, home of the Scuppernong grape. The name survived in various non-alcoholic forms during Prohibition, and well beyond although the Scuppernong flavour had to be diluted with California grapes as so many North Carolina vineyards disappeared for good in the 1920s. Garrett spent 62 years in the wine trade and was a founder of the modern industry in the US.

16. 'Foxy' is a term used to describe the wines made from *Vitis labrusca* grapes, a species native to America and chiefly grown commercially in the vineyards of the East Coast. These grapes have a distinctive musky, perfumy aroma which can be appreciably lessened when they are crossed with European *Vitis vinifera* varieties. Concord grapes are the most pungent example of this scent – they are used to make wines (usually sweet in style) as well as grape-juice and jellies.

17. The use of willow hoops is traditional in Burgundy. No doubt they are used in other areas as well but rarely, if ever, in Bordeaux.

Tips of the (Wine) Trade

1. Alas, one can only value it as a curiosity, as the quality of the brandy will only be known after the bottle has been opened and the contents tasted. Cognac brandy or, indeed, any other spirit does not improve in bottle, only in wood and preferably in small oak barrels. Thus to be able to value an old bottle of cognac, one must know how long it has spent in wood before being bottled.

2. It is a style of wine named 'Moseltaler'. Like Liebfraumilch it must be a *Qualität* wine (QbA) and thus be the product of one *Anbaugebiet* within the Mosel area; the residual sugar must be between 15 and 30 grams per litre and the total acidity not less than 7 grams per litre. The restricted grape varieties are Riesling, Müller-Thurgau,

Elbling and Kerner. The more the Riesling, the slatier the vineyard, the better the Moseltaler. Like Liebfraumilch, it can be marketed under any merchant's brand.

The famous portrait of Mme ('Veuve') Cliquot who managed with such success the business which bears her name.

3. (a) Veuve Clicquot is the widow who at a very young age took over the management of the champagne house that bears her name, following the unfortunate death of her husband. Her personal reputation is as high as that of her wine, because she reputedly invented *remuage*. Apparently, it remained a long and well-kept secret.
(b) Sticky green is the much loved Crème de Menthe.

4. Today, only vintage ports and all Alsatian wines. Frankly, all the rest are likely to be bottled in the area of production, but need not legally be. Spanish sherry could very easily not be bottled in Spain – whereby hangs a story. We were interviewing a possible shop manager. His credentials suggested he had been *maître d'hôtel* in most of North America's finest restaurants. We enquired if we might ask him some wine questions. 'Anything, anything,' he replied with total confidence. The first and alas, the last question was: 'Where does Tio Pepe Sherry come from?'

His reply, which fascinated us all, was 'Persia'. In our astonishment, we had of course forgotten there is a place called Shiraz in Iran, which sort of made sense.

5. 1978 – when there was a reclassification of most of the *crus bourgeois* of the Médoc. They were subdivided as follows:

  i.   *Cru bourgeois*
  ii. *Cru grand bourgeois*
  iii. *Cru grand bourgeois exceptionel*

One has to assume that the English translation of *bourgeois* does not equate to that of France. Why should the French apparently wish to call a group of highly respectable (some even classy) wines the equivalent of 'home-spun and dull'?

There used to be *crus artisans* which seems to have disappeared. It is a pity, as *artisan* in either language is a nice word which suggests rolled-up sleeves and a wish to get on.

6. Again the answer is 'Wines' with the added information – such imports come mostly from Spain and Algiers.

We are speaking of the earliest 1900s when it was quite impossible for France to satisfy her café *vin ordinaire* trade with her own wines (in fact one wonders if she can, even today). Also at that time the lighter clarets, if they were to stand up to any form of travel, needed to be mildly fortified with stronger wines. Obviously as wine knowledge increased, such strengthening became unnecessary.

7. Correct as regards sherries. Sherries are the epitome of blending, and their labels show no age or date. The vast majority of wood ports are also blends and there is no way

of knowing their exact age. But fine old blends of wood port can be awarded an age by strict and expert tasting. One can submit samples of old blends (invariably tawnies) to the *Instituto Do Vinho Do Porto* who will test and taste the wine and award it an age certificate. This age may appear on the label but the latter must also state that the port has been matured in wood and the date on which it was bottled. The age award can even reach 40 years.

Wood port and vintage port are as different as Bordeaux and Burgundy and, like the two latter, each have their firmest devotees. As the name suggests, wood port matures in wood and, when bottled, is ready to drink. Exactly like sherry, it is best served from the wood into the glass, which is obviously impractical, but storing wood port in bottle is usually a disappointing exercise.

Such ports are all blends (there is one exception) and, like sherry, their exact age is impossible to date. They start their life as full, mauve ruby port and, as they mature in oak pipes (116 imperial/139.3 US gallons), their colour changes to a gentle, russet tawny. At least, that is the theory, but in this life one gets what one pays for. Certainly most port houses market at least one fine tawny made in this manner and very splendid wines they are, but understandably expensive. A light, fully acceptable tawny to match one's pocket ('schoolboy port' according to some of the older generation) is usually a blend of red and white wines.

A port sample room in Vila Nova de Gaia after a blind tasting.

Today, people are more conscious of vintage. It is now possible to bottle a port of one vintage which has aged in wood for a minimum of eight years. The label will show the vintage, the date of bottling and the vital fact the port has been aged in wood. It is not a traditional vintage port.

Traditional vintage port spends approximately two years in wood and the remainder of its life in bottle. In a great vintage, its life span is longer than that of the average port consumer. Vintage port is bottled (by law, only in Portugal) complete with all its deposit which it has not had time to shed in wood. With so many options available, it is silly to drink vintage port before it is at least ten years old. By this time, it will have 'thrown' its deposit in bottle and decanting is a must.

Many people prefer not to wait, and regard decanting

as a ritualistic performance. They are very well served by late-bottled vintage port, which will have spent double the time of vintage port in wood and so shed much of its deposit and will also be ready to drink far earlier. Today, these excellent and convenient (not meant in a derogatory sense) ports are usually bottled deposit-free and need no decanting.

Vintage ports are bottled with the longest corks in the business. The easiest way to extract them is to use an old fashioned cork-screw with quite a long point at the end of the curly part. There are two very fancy alternatives. One is a pair of hot tongs which clasps the neck of the bottle and burns off cork and glass as one entity. The second, is

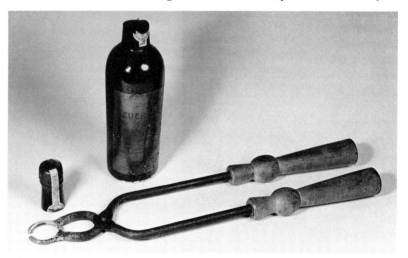

A bottle of vintage port successfully decapitated with red-hot tongs.

to give the neck of the bottle (just below the cork) a firm, sharp tap with a steel knife which should cause a clean break, again with glass and cork as one entity. This last method was recently demonstrated by someone reputedly skilled in such practices at a port seminar – it is a true story. The tap against the neck of the bottle was duly administered. It had no effect on the neck but the bottom 'punt' of the bottle plus port fell to the floor. It was later explained that there must have been some fault in the bottle, but it caused much amusement among those present.

8. Many buyers of Bordeaux châteaux wines (primarily classified growths) buy such wines as soon as they are

released by the château. It is usually not possible to buy directly from the château and the order is placed via a merchant. Over the years (1972/4 were exceptions), this has proved a very profitable way of buying Bordeaux, whether for investment or normal trading. Even so, such style of buying is more and more the norm and perhaps some of the cream has disappeared.

A château will normally offer a proportion of its wine of the last vintage around March/April following that vintage. This is the first *tranche*, each succeeding *tranche* becoming more expensive. The château may sell at a bulk price when the unit of sale is the *tonneau* = four *barriques* = 96 dozen bottles. There will be two invoices for payment of that sale by the end of the year. All further charges of bottling, storage, insurance and shipment, etc. will then be charged about three years later when the wine is delivered. Today, many châteaux simplify the procedure and charge not in bulk in the first instance, but per dozen bottles and again ancillary charges are paid on delivery. Regular trade buyers are normally subject to a form of conditional trading by those châteaux who never have difficulty in selling their total crop in 'good years'. Such châteaux expect their regular buyers to buy in 'off years' if the latter expect to obtain their full quota in the better years. At this moment in time (March 1987), the advantages of *'en primeur'* buying must be in the balance. The moderate 1984 is basically unsold wherever it is lying, while all of the great 1985 which Bordeaux has been prepared to release is sold but not yet bottled, and now there is a very large and good 1986 vintage which has not yet been released. The sixty-four thousand dollar question is, will the opening prices of Bordeaux classified growths 1986 be lower than for the same wines when they opened in 1985?

There was a time (not today) when it was not uncommon to buy *'sur souche'* which meant buying one's requirements before the grapes had been picked. One bought perhaps in June and took the extra gamble and paid less. The last time we did this, we were also in Bordeaux at the moment of the vintage and everything was as it should be – ripe grapes, ideal weather, and so on. Driving towards Calais, the car almost found its own way to a Michelin three star set-up for an obvious celebration. The *sommelier*, alas, took the gilt off the gingerbread by asking if we had heard the news. France had just devalued the Franc!

9.   i.   Table wine – *Deutscher Tafelwein*
     ii. Quality wine – *Qualitätswein*
     iii. Extra quality wine – *Qualitätswein mit Prädikat*

Deutscher Tafelwein is an all-German wine made from grapes grown in one of five regions which are based on the German wine rivers – Mosel, Rhein, Main, Neckar and Oberrhein. These wines will be labelled with the river and possibly *Bereich* name plus usually a brand name. Their grape-juice will almost certainly have been sugared to obtain more alcohol (prior to winemaking) and limited blending between the five areas is allowed. A Rhein *Tafelwein* can therefore contain Mosel.

Qualitätswein must be the product of grapes grown totally in one of the following designated areas and no blending between the areas may take place. In German these eleven areas are known as *Anbaugebiete*, and *Qualitätswein* is normally shortened to QbA standing for *Qualitätswein bestimmter Anbaugebiete*. The areas are:

(a) Ahr: northern tributary of the Rhein
(b) Hessische Bergstrasse: east of Rheinhessen, west of Franken
(c) Mittelrhein: south of Ahr but still northern Rhine
(d) Mosel-Saar-Ruwer: The Mosel from Koblenz to Trier plus the tributaries Saar south of and Ruwer north of Trier
(e) Nahe: south of Rheingau, west of Rheinhessen
(f) Rheingau: The very cream of the Rheinland
(g) Rheinhessen: larger than Rheingau and south of it
(h) Rheinpfalz (Palatinate): greater output and again south
(i) Franken (Franconia): eastern Rheinland
(j) Württemberg: based on the river Neckar, further south
(k) Baden: Germany's most southern wine district

Like *Tafelwein*, QbA wines may have their musts (grape-juice) sugared. But before they can be labelled *Quali-*

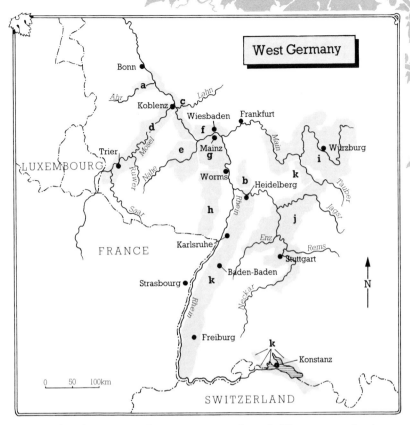

Wine Regions

a Ahr
b Hessische Bergstrasse
c Mittelrhein
d Mosel-Saar-Ruwer
e Nahe
f Rheingau
g Rheinhessen
h Rheinpfalz
i Franken
j Württemberg
k Baden

tätswein, they must be taste-tested and, if approved, given a number (basically a code of the wine's ancestry) which will appear on the label. It is always referred to as the AP number (short for *Amtliche Prüfungsnummer*). All wines from now on up to the highest quality will be labelled with an AP number.

Qualitätswein mit Prädikat (QmP)

The Germans first grade their wines by *Oechsle* scale which measures the sugar in the must, and so the potential alcohol produced by fermentation. *Qualitätswein mit Prädikat* (QmP) wines may not have sugar added to their musts to increase the alcohol. But each *Anbaugebiet* issues a schedule which shows how much must, sugar and alcohol the wine must have to obtain each *Prädikat* grade. The *Prädikats* available are:

(a) *Kabinett*: better than average wine, the grapes of which are gathered at the normal time of harvest.

May be blended with wines from the same *Anbaugebiet*.

(b) *Spätlese*: wines made from late-harvested grapes which have started to shrivel and concentrate their sugar. From now onwards QmP wines can only be blended with wines from their own *Bereich* (an area within the *Anbaugebiet*).

(c) *Auslese*: bunches of grapes picked individually at their peak of ripeness.

(d) *Beerenauslese*: individual berries picked as they are becoming over-ripe. '*Edelfäule*' or noble rot will be in evidence.

(e) *Trockenbeerenauslese*: only individual berries are picked which have definitely been affected by noble rot. One is told, it may take a single picker a full day to pick enough berries eventually to make a single bottles-worth of wine.

(f) *Eiswein*: is not in itself a *Prädikat* but is an additional description to *auslesen* wine, denoting the grapes have been picked and pressed (even as late as the January following the vintage) while the bunch is completely frozen. It is of course only the water content of the grape which freezes, greatly raising the degree of sweetness.

Snow on grapes in Germany.

The above three main categories, plus only six words denoting stages of quality, were the initial opening move to do away with an absurd superfluity of 'home-made' labels which made it almost impossible to market the better-quality German wines, prior to 1971.

The next move was to divide each *Anbaugebiet* into a *Bereich* which is a large area of similar wines. The *Bereich* is divided into smaller areas named *Grosslagen*, which in turn are divided into individual vineyards called *Einzellagen*.

All new wine laws are constantly added to or amended, the German laws of 1971 prove the point.

10. Each *barrique* is not bottled independently. Theoretically, all the barrels are blended together to make one château wine, but it would be totally exceptional for a serious château to bottle the entire crop under the château label.

A dedicated château owner makes the highest quality wine he can afford. To be extreme, it is possible that the average cost of producing one case of château X could be double, or conversely half, the price of producing the next door château's one case – even though both estates have the identical *appellation*. A few of the most expensive ways of achieving the highest quality wine from one château are:

i. To restrict the yield taken from each acre of vineyard.
ii. Each year, to store the total harvest in new oak *barriques*.
iii. Prior to bottling, to discard all wine which falls below the top quality of the château. The discarded wine is then sold at the applicable *appellation* or (and this is increasingly the pattern) is used in the château's second or even third wine.

11. False. It is normal for the Burgundies, Romanée-Conti and La Tâche to fetch higher prices than most claret – one assumes in either case the vintage is acceptable. Auction prices are quoted in various trade magazines and the following prices at recent (February 1987) auctions are shown in round figures as follows. All wines quoted are per dozen duty paid, vintage 1976.

Average price of the Bordeaux first growths	£380 ($578)
Price of Château Petrus	£900 ($1368)
Price of Romanée-Conti	£1650 ($2508)
Price of La Tâche	£820 ($1246)

Are we comparing apples and oranges? No, we are comparing Bordeaux and Burgundy which, maybe, is the same thing. Burgundy has any amount of small vineyards each carefully classified and with their own *appellation*. Admittedly, Romanée-Conti is exceptional (in everything – not just size) being just about five acres. The average classified Bordeaux château must be (but I don't know) twenty times that size.

Bordeaux in a normal year produces at least double the gallonage of all Burgundy plus Beaujolais. It can therefore claim that at its highest level of quality (not just any Bordeaux), it produces in quantity the finest red wines in the world. California may well dissent. At the same highest level of quality, Bordeaux can equally claim to be the producer of the greatest sweet table wines in the world. Germany will obviously disagree but is short on quantity.

Burgundy, speaking again only of the highest quality, produces the finest dry white wines of the world. California dissenting even more vociferously. One discusses only the highest quality wines because one judges a country's wine by the best it can produce. No country in the world wins at all levels.

12. The overall answer is the year the grapes were harvested but, like everything else in the wine world, there are exceptions. With reference to vintage, the exception is *Eiswein*. Eiswein grapes were picked in mid-January 1980 at 10° Celsius. The vintage will be shown as 1979.

13. This 'e' is required on wine and food alike. It means that the quantity stated has been checked and certified. The bottle in the picture has been filled to 70 cl.

14. Except for very old wines, the answer must generally be 'yes', provided the wine has a few weeks rest at the receiving end. The days are passed when wines no longer 'travel well'.

Admittedly, there is a very strong case for stating that all wine tastes better in the area of production. But how can that be proved? It was certainly refuted recently by a very notable winemaker who stated emphatically that his own wines tasted the same the world over. Someone then suggested that as wine was a living thing it might perhaps suffer some temporary sickness through travel. The winemaker replied that he was never travelsick, the obvious inference being his children (his wines) would not be either. Obviously, wines can get sick not by travel but their own metabolism and similarly cure themselves. They occasionally just go through a bad period.

One of the joys of visiting the various wine areas is that one can be served an amazingly old wine in perfect condition but only because it has never left its original cellar.

What's in a Name

1. (a) Les Vaucrains is one of the major first growth vineyards of Nuits-St-Georges.

(b) Vaucluse is a French Department in the Rhône Valley. It houses such names as Gigondas, Châteauneuf-du-Pape and Côtes du Ventoux.

(c) The Volstead Act brought in prohibition in the United States in 1920.

(d) Valais is a still-flourishing vineyard area in southern Switzerland with the Rhône as its northern border. Two of us will always remember Valais for a slightly strange reason.

The scene is a Swiss restaurant, the time of year, a week or two before the release of Beaujolais Nouveau. As we sat down, we saw 'tent cards' on each table announcing '*Le Beaujolais Nouveau est arrivé*'. This could not be true, and we asked to see the bottle. Astonishing – 'Beaujolais Nouveau' produced and bottled in Switzerland. We obviously queried it. The restaurateur looked pained. 'Why, sir, do you mention Beaujolais, this is not Beaujolais?' Nor was it. Both the 'tent cards' and the label were clearly printed 'Beau Valais Nouveau'. Such is the power of auto-suggestion – and neither of us had had a glass of anything.

2. They are all *vins de pays* denominated zones.

3. (a) Grinzing, location Austria and about a tram's drive from Vienna. The village wine excites with its '*nouveau*', known locally as 'Heurige'.

(b) Grumello, location Italy, the Province of Lombardy in the Valtellina valley. Grumello, Sassella and Inferno are all areas producing similar wines made primarily from the Chiavennasca (Nebbiolo) grape and they all make very pleasant drinking.

(c) Grèves: one of the major first growths of Beaune. Drinkable at an early age but better to keep for its ever-increasing round, velvety warmth. This is a wine normally easy to appreciate – *facile à boire*.

(d) Grenouilles is one of the seven *grand crus* of Chablis. It is Chardonnay at its sternest best.

4. The five vineyards concerned are: Clos de la Roche, Clos de Tart, Clos des Lambrays, Clos St Denis and, probably the best known, Clos de Vougeot which reputedly has more owners than hectares causing the quality perhaps to be variable. All these vineyards are *grand cru* and all have their own *appellation* – thus Clos de Tart is classified as *Appellation Clos de Tart Controlée*.

Strangely, four of these vineyards (Clos de Vougeot being the exception) are situated in the commune of Morey St Denis in the Côte de Nuits and there must be a reason for this. Perhaps long ago there was a quarry in the area which made enclosure-building easy – only a wild guess.

Many of us wonder why the word *domaine* is never included in the AOC and as *clos* has been, why only five?

It may make things clearer to name a few similar wines with their actual *appellations*.

Clos L'Église:	AOC Pomerol, area Bordeaux
Clos de la Poussie:	AOC Sancerre, area Loire
Clos de la Commaraine:	AOC Pommard, *premier cru*, area Burgundy
Domaine de Chevalier:	AOC Graves, *grand cru*, Bordeaux
Domaine de Nalys:	AOC Châteauneuf-du-Pape, southern Rhône.

5. Pouilly is not an appellation anywhere, it is a village in the Loire valley and a commune in Burgundy. Even so, there are five AC French wines, each prefixed Pouilly:

Pouilly-Fuissé: made from the grape Chardonnay, it is usually the highest quality of the three Pouilly wines in the Mâconnais in southern Burgundy. It is rather a preserve of the USA, which is interesting. More often, when a wine gains great popularity in a foreign country, it is the pronunciation of its name which plays the major part. Pouilly-Fuissé is certainly not easy to pronounce. The British chose Beaune and Chablis and prefer to call Bordeaux, claret.

Pouilly-Loché and *Pouilly-Vinzelles:* both are able to supply delightful Chardonnay wines and are usually less expensive than the Fuissé.

A map for visitors showing the tour of the vineyards of Pouilly-Fuissé.

Pouilly-Fumé: is a very popular dry wine at the extreme eastern tip of the Val de Loire. The taste is reputedly evocative of 'gun-flint' which is a very old and rather strange simile for the Sauvignon grape. It has not got the 'staying power' in bottle of its Burgundy namesakes.

Pouilly-sur-Loire: is from the same area as the Fumé, but made from the Chasselas grape which, we are told, may sooner or later disappear from the area.

6. The clue lies in the spelling – Madera is a county in the hot Central Valley of California which has more than 30,000 acres of vineyards mostly intended for table wines. It is also the home of Ficklin port, made from traditional Portuguese varieties such as Souzao, which is generally reckoned by tasters to be a well-made wine, if not exactly port as made in Europe.

7. It is a wine but not German, it is Alsatian which obviously, in the past, has been German more than once.

Alsace, one of the most enchanting corners of France (Riquewihr is pure Disneyland), goes in for what has become known as 'varietal' labelling. They label their wines with the grape from which the wine has been 100 per cent made. The *appellation* Alsace remains constant no matter what the grape variety. The word Edelzwicker is the exception to the one-grape wine; it is a blend of any of the grapes allowed for the *appellation* Alsace.

The varietal grape names of Alsace are Sylvaner, Pinot Blanc, Muscat, Tokay, Pinot Gris, Gewürztraminer and Riesling – probably in rising order of nobility. Those are the grapes with which the non-Alsatian is familiar – there are one or two others.

To the Alsatian, as indeed to the German, the Riesling is the noblest of grapes, but in very basic, simplistic terms the Alsatian Riesling is dry, most other Rieslings are sweet – from Germany to California via other wine countries.

It frustrates the Alsatian that his adored Riesling is not necessarily adored by all his export friends. Frankly, there is a certain severity in a young Alsatian Riesling but they should not be drunk young. There still lingers in the back of people's minds that appalling phrase, 'White wines must be drunk young'. It is totally wrong for quality white wines, and the Alsatian Riesling very much proves the point.

Gewürztraminer must be the most popular (price prevents it being the best seller) of all Alsatian wines worldwide. It should be popular – at its best, it is the finest Gewürztraminer made; at its less good, it is still easy to recognize. For a consumer to recognize what he is drinking, after a couple of sniffs, must give it a head-start over other wines!

All Alsatian wines are vinified dry (even Muscat) unless they are late gathered (*vendange tardive*) or even later gathered and the berries, possibly affected by *Botrytis*, individually picked. This latter rarity used to use the German name *Beerenauslese* even *Trockenbeerenauslese*. Today, thanks to the Hugel family, it is officially described as '*Sélection des Grains Nobles*'.

What is puzzling to many of us is that the extreme southern end of German Rheinland is pretty well within walking distance of the Alsace vineyards, yet German dry wines (*trocken* and *halbtrocken*) have difficulty matching the dry wines of Alsace. To taste the fruit in a dry wine, one needs alcohol. The Alsatians are allowed a higher degree of chaptalization than the southern Germans, but that isn't the answer because a *grand cru* Alsatian wine will reach 11 per cent alcohol with no chaptalization. The most telling factor is almost certainly the 'backcloth' of the Vosges mountains, making Alsace one of the driest and hottest (in summer) areas of France.

8. (a) *Floraison* is when the vine flowers produce tiny green berries. Bad weather conditions can cause these flower-berries to fall off and so cut down the eventual weight of grapes. In Bordeaux, the Merlot which flowers before the Cabernet Sauvignon, suffered this way in 1984. It was cold and the sap shrank back, giving no sustenance to the flowers and the Merlot crop partially failed. Curiously, whenever there is frost or similar damage in the vineyards, the poor sap gets the blame – when it should be up, it's down, or the other way round.

One of the rough yardsticks in the vineyard is that the harvest follows 100 days after flowering.

(b) *Veraison* usually arrives about a couple of months after *floraison* when both black and white grapes start to change their colour and look like their final selves.

9. (a) Ullage is the space between the wine and the top of its container – barrel or bottle. Most wines maturing in barrel require the barrel to be absolutely full and are regularly topped up, so that there is no ullage between the wine and the top of the barrel and thus no unnecessary oxidation. Most wine bottles are stored horizontally so that the wine and cork are in contact and the latter does not dry thin and allow air into the bottle.

(b) Not easy to define, but in military terms it literally means a cadet thus in wine terms it means a lesser-quality wine.

(c) A *venencia* is used primarily in the *bodegas* of Jerez de la Frontera to obtain a cupful of clear *fino* from under its

The courtyard of the Hospices de Beaune which auctions the wines from its vineyards every year – certainly the most famous annual wine sale.

covering of *flor*. It can be made of anything, but traditionally is a length of whalebone with a narrow silver cup at the business end and often a silver hook at the other end with which to hang it up. It is fascinating to watch a skilled Spanish cellarman plunge his *venencia* through the 'flor' and fill one *'copita'* (sherry glass) from the highest range. It is miraculous to see him do the same into a number of glasses held in the other hand – never spilling a drop.

(d) *Les Trois Glorieuses* relate to the three banquets held during the weekend at the end of November when the Hospices de Beaune auctions the bulk wine (of the immediate past harvest) from its own properties.

The Hospices de Beaune (itself one of the glories of the city) is a fifteenth century charitable hospital. It no longer houses the old and sick, but still cares for them elsewhere. Over the centuries, it has been endowed with plots of vineyards and it is the product of these vineyards which is auctioned.

The third weekend of November is when Beaune is host to the wine merchants of the world. To buy at the sale of the Hospices de Beaune is to get one's name in wine magazines, the world over, to meet a global wine fraternity-sorority and to help a charity. The prices reached at the auction are pointers towards other Burgundy prices of the same vintage. The average prices of 1986 were appreciably lower than the extremely high prices of the previous year. The actual banquets are:

Saturday	Dinner hosted by the *Chevaliers du Tastevin* at Clos de Vougeot
Sunday	Dinner (after the auction) at the Hospices
Monday	Luncheon at Meursault known as La Paulée

10. All German wines labelled *trocken* have indeed been vinified dry. In fact there are three classifications of German dry wines:

i. *Trocken-diabetiker*: maximum sugar, 4 grams per litre
ii. *Trocken*: maximum sugar between 5 and 9 grams per litre
iii. *Halbtrocken* (half-dry): sugar between 10 and 18 grams per litre

Trockenbeerenauslese is the highest *Prädikat* one can give to all that is most noble in a German wine and is enormously high in natural grape sugar. Let us dissect the word and so understand why *trocken* forms part of Germany's sweetest wine. *Trockenbeeren*, literally means 'dry berries', but in the sense of 'dried-up berries'; *auslese* means 'selected'. Thus the word *Trockenbeerenauslese* means 'selected dried-up berries'. In fact the berries have been dried up and made raisin-like with all their sugar concentrated by *Botrytis*. The pickers in the vineyards have to select individual berries and ignore any that are not totally shrivelled. It may take one picker twelve hours to collect enough grapes to make 75 cl of wine!

Let us revert to *trocken* wines in the dry sense. All German '*Landwein*' which is produced in fifteen large areas and equates to the French *vin du pays*, may not be sweeter than *halbtrocken*. The Germans now realize that the public are turning to genuine dry wines and the old days of talking dry and drinking sweet are finished. But are they making a success of these *trocken* and *halbtrocken* wines? So many countries are climatically better equipped to make reasonably high-alcohol dry white wines than Germany. But no other country can make the German style of wine with that astonishing balance of sugar and acid which makes a sweet wine taste so full of fruit that it is almost dry. I happen to be a great believer in 'horses for courses'.

11. *Tastevinage* is a function organized by the *Confrérie des Chevaliers du Tastevin de Bourgogne*. Before giving you the details and purpose of this function, it might be helpful first to explain the affairs of the *Confrérie* to those who are unfamiliar with the set-up.

The *Confrérie des Chevaliers du Tastevin* is a brotherhood or club dedicated to the promotion of Burgundy wines world-wide. Everything connected with it can only be described in superlatives. Its headquarters are housed in the ancient Cistercian monastery of Clos de Vougeot, much renovated but always in perfect taste, the total ambience idyllic.

Most wine areas the world over have their 'promotional societies' (with funny hats, etc.), but the membership of the *Chevaliers du Tastevin* and what they achieve internationally must surpass all the others put together.

The main attractions offered to their members and guests are about a dozen banquets a year, staged at Clos de Vougeot. Banquets are not normally associated with fine dining. However, the *Chevaliers du Tastevin* banquet (for 500 plus) would satisfy any gourmet or indeed gourmand –

with wines to complement each course. One knows the Burgundian *appellation* of each wine and its vintage but not the 'maker'. The *Confrérie* promotes Burgundy wine not directly any Burgundy firm.

Admittedly, the evening is long, with songs we now all know and French tongue-twister jokes and extremely erudite speeches we will never understand but we still laugh at the former and applaud the latter.

The length of the evening has the great advantage of enabling one to drive home happy but competent, though should any gendarme be so ill-advised as to breathalyse any driver on the night of a *Chevalier* dinner, he would surely find himself smartly transferred to the Bordeaux force.

The insignia of the *Confrérie* is the *tastevin* – a shallow open silver cup with a convenient handle (ancient ones often have crossed snakes' heads as handles) which the locals use for tasting wine. The inside of the cup has round and long indentations. One judges the colour of red wines in the round indentations and the shade of white wines in the long ones (it may be the other way round, as I don't use them!) and then one sips and spits. I suspect one must be brought up from an early age to taste this way. For an ordinary mortal, a glass makes the job far easier. Even so, it is still commonplace to descend into some small bulk cellar and for the owner to taste each cask with a *tastevin* which may well have been previously used by three or four generations of his family.

Back at long last to the *tastevinage*. The *Confrérie* organize annually (or biannually), and often immediately prior to the sale of wines at the Hospices de Nuits St Georges, a tasting to pick out wines of the highest quality relative to their *appellation* and vintage. Wines judged by the jury to have achieved this distinction are awarded a *Tasteviné* label. This label will show the *appellation*, the vintage, the name of the shipper, in fact everything a normal label will show, but it will bear the very distinguished crest of the *Confrérie*, proving that the wine has been approved by the jury of the *tastevinage*. The jury is made up of independent wine merchants at every level and indeed anyone with professional wine interests. There are always a few representatives from other countries. Normally, there are six jurors to each table who very soon fall into the spirit of a team, organizing their own method of tasting the bottles for which they are responsible. The tasting is blind only as regards the supplier; the *appellation* and the vintage has to be known. The only limit to the age of the wine is that it must have a minimum of six months' bottle age – there is no maximum age limit. I have only been a juror once, in 1975, which was great fun and I hope to do it again. In 1975 there were 463 lots and a success rate of 57.5 per cent. This is lower than the average which is usually in the sixties, but the number of lots today has reached more than a thousand.

12. All four expressions are designed to tell the reader that the vineyard, the maturing of its grapes and finally their bottling have been controlled by the owner of the vineyard and many people add, 'which is a guarantee of authenticity'. Personally, I take exception to this latter remark as all bottling, wherever it takes place (even out of the country of origin), is authentic, so long as the wine merchant is authentic, which happily is the norm. Having got that off my chest, one must admit that the public seem to accept it as some form of guarantee that other types of bottling do not have.

(a) In more detail, *mis en bouteilles au château* (MC for short) means exactly what it says, and is primarily associated with Bordeaux. But other wine châteaux exist in France where the whole operation from grape to bottle takes place within the confines of a château, and who therefore use the phrase.

(b) The word *domaine* has no legal backing as to meaning or size. It is just a bit of land and you can call it what you like – but *domaine* bottled has a significance. It literally means the owner of the vineyard has been responsible for the bottling of the wine. Perhaps it is most associated with Burgundy but is used all over France. Usually the *domaine* has no bottling facilities at the vineyard site and therefore the wine is matured and bottled in the owner's cellars. Sometimes the vineyard owner has no bottling facilities at all, merely old-world cellars and great expertise in rearing wine, after all plenty of business tycoons can't work the computer. Such vineyard owners hire a travelling bottling plant (they are normally highly efficient) which parks outside his 'back door' and *domaine* bottles his wine.

(c) Bottling at the property is the most difficult to explain. It sounds exactly the same as bottling at the château and is often printed across a label in a way to suggest just that – but it isn't château bottling. Perhaps its main significance is that if the vineyard owner is a member of the local co-operative, he can legally claim his wine has been bottled at the property, although the actual bottling was in fact done by the co-operative.

(d) Finally the German word '*Erzeugerabfullung*' is translated 'estate bottled', again meaning the owner of the vineyard has also bottled the wine. But similarly to the French, if the bottling has been done by his local co-operative, it is still described as estate bottled.

13. *Landwein* was introduced in Germany in 1982 to match the *vin de pays* of France. It is a German table wine with geographical connections. There are in fact only fifteen designated areas where *Landwein* may be produced and the style of the wine, although corresponding to other wines coming from the same area, will always be on the dry side. *Landwein* must be *trocken* or *halbtrocken* which means its sweetness will not exceed 18 grams of residual sugar per litre.

This particular *Landwein* comes from the Saar, a tributary of the Mosel.

 **IV**

The Fizz Quiz

1. The wine is French champagne which was granted the AC in 1936, and indeed was favoured with some other legal protection prior to that date. This fact is never shown on the label, but is a legal obligation on all other French AC wines. May we call that oddity no. 1.

Oddity no. 2: champagne may legally blend red and white wines together to make rosé. Disallowed to all other rosés. Admittedly champagne also uses the more traditional maceration method. (Maceration in relation to rosé wines means that the black grapes have been allowed to ferment on their skins for a short time causing the resultant wine to be pink.)

May we digress – the late but very great André Simon who knew more about champagne than I have had hot dinners (or whatever the expression is) once told me an easier recipe for making pink champagne. 'My young friend,' he said (and it might have been Maurice Chevalier speaking) 'just let fall a few drops of cochineal into the bottle of your favourite champagne and voilà you have pink champagne. The mousse will quickly mix it all up, but do not shake the bottle, allow the mousse to do it, otherwise you'll think you've won the Reims Grand Prix.'

I have done it (with real cochineal) and it works. There is a further advantage in that cochineal is a tasteless dye and therefore does not affect the flavour of the champagne of your choice.

Oddity no. 3: many champagnes are made from a far greater quantity of black grapes (Pinot Noir and Meunier) than white (Chardonnay). Yet there is no such thing as French red champagne.

The only *appellations* of champagne are:

Champagne	Sparkling or half-sparkling (*crémant*). A white or rosé wine made only from the grapes Pinot Noir, Pinot Meunier and Chardonnay. Usually, a blend of black and white grapes, often all white grapes, Chardonnay (*blanc de blancs*), and occasionally all black grapes (*blanc de noirs*).
Rosé des Riceys	A rosé wine made only from the Pinot Noir grape.
Coteaux Champenois	Covers red, white and rosé still wines from the legally defined Champagne area and replaces the previous description 'Champagne Nature' which is no longer legal.

2. The village is Bouzy producing black grapes and rated 100 per cent in Champagne's unique pricing arrangements. Bouzy's grapes may help to make up a *cuvée* of champagne or a still red Coteaux Champenois.

Most champagne houses (whatever vineyards they may own) buy grapes from growers. The price they pay is partially determined by a long-standing 'rating' of the village in which they were grown. The top villages (Bouzy, Sillery and Cramant are three examples) are rated 100 per cent. The lowest rating is 80 per cent. Prior to the champagne harvest and of necessity (ripeness of the grapes, etc.) dangerously near to it, a committee of buyers and grape farmers meet to fix the price per kilo of grapes for the approaching crop. Grapes from those villages rated 100 per cent get the full price, villages rated lower fetch their percentage-worth. It is on that basis that one bargains. Obviously every year, various circumstances make adjustments necessary.

3. No such wine exists. If the description *blanc de blancs* is meant to suggest something exceptional, it really is a bit of a 'con', as in practice it expresses the norm, but possibly may increase sales without hurting anyone.

4. (a) *Remuage* is common to both areas. One can still see it done by hand in Champagne, but machines are taking over more and more and indeed have pretty well taken over in Spain.
(b) The predominance of black grapes applies only to Champagne. In Catalonia, white grapes comfortably predominate.
(c) The chalky soil plays a prominent part in both areas. In Champagne, it is the Kimmeridge clay (also found in Chablis). In Catalonia, it is the Albariza chalk – our old friend from Jerez de la Frontera.

5. Champagne. Perhaps an *aide-mémoire* on the *'méthode champenoise'* is the simplest way to explain it all.

The first essential of the champagne process is a second fermentation in bottle. Ideally, the bottle in which this second fermentation takes place is the same bottle that eventually reaches the public. Sizes smaller than a half bottle or larger than a magnum are usually decanted under pressure.

By April following the vintage, the *cuvée* (the blend

A remueur *rattling and angling the yeast deposit on to the first closure of bottles of champagne* – remuage.

The highlighted yeast deposit in champagne after the second fermentation in bottle.

of wines selected by the champagne house) is ready for bottling.

To ensure a second fermentation will occur in the bottle, the *'liqueur de tirage'* is added. This is a solution of sugar, wine and selected yeasts. The yeasts will feed on the sugar, creating alcohol and carbon dioxide.

For two or three years, the wine matures, the bottles being stacked in the horizontal position.

When the wine approaches the time for sale to the public, the bottle has to be opened in order to get rid of the dead yeast cells which have now formed a deposit. The wine will also invariably have to be sweetened.

The first step is *remuage*, the process of shaking the bottle either by hand or machine until the deposit rests on the base of the first closure, usually a metal cap, still sometimes a cork.

By the time this is fully completed, the bottle will be in

A typical pupitre *holding bottles for the action of* remuage.

the perpendicular position and is stacked that way, each bottle head down.

The final operations start with *dégorgement*, the process of getting rid of the sediment by placing the bottle, still standing on its head, in a freezing mixture which solidifies the deposit. The bottle is then opened and the pellet of frozen deposit is blown out of the bottle by the carbon dioxide, i.e. the fizz of the champagne.

Dosage immediately follows; the wine is sweetened by a 'dose' of *liqueur d'expedition*, a blend of sugar, brandy and champagne. It is rare for champagnes not to receive some sweetening although Brut (the driest) usually receives less than 1 per cent. The bottle is then recorked with surprisingly large, high-quality corks and clamped down with a wire cage. *Dégorgement, dosage, liqueur d'expedition* and, finally, corking are one continuous operation – now totally mechanical but closely following what used to be done by the skill of a cellarman. Years ago, I was allowed to try *dégorgement* by hand. After the second attempt, everyone ran for cover.

Obviously, after this somewhat drastic treatment, the wine has to be rested before labelling and despatch.

On reaching its various markets, it is ready to drink. It should be stored horizontally like any other wine, but theoretically does not improve in bottle. However, it will certainly change its character and many people prefer 'old' champagne. It is easy to tell whether a champagne was disgorged two or three years ago (apart from colour and taste) by the cork. The narrower and harder the cork, the longer the period since *dégorgement*; the more mushroom-like the cork, the opposite. There was a time when many British wine merchants liked to sell their champagnes 'old-landed', meaning the wine had been sitting in bond for about nine months, and the cork had started to narrow – not today.

This brings us back (at last) to the question. If a champagne (invariably a vintage wine) is not disgorged but left standing on its head, the wine quietly ages on the yeast for an extremely long time – the blockage of yeast deposit between cork and wine plays its part. Most champagne houses carry a stock of such wine, which is disgorged only when required. In the area of production, the wine could date back to 1911, and certainly in the early 1980s in London one could buy the famous 1928 vintage which had been recently disgorged. Needless to say, the normal 1928 vintage, disgorged whenever it was (maybe 1934), would almost certainly have died long ago. There is one minor snag which is that these very old wines which have recently been disgorged are not for keeping and, once open, cannot be lingered over.

The House of Bollinger specializes in rather older vintages which have been recently disgorged, and I am pretty sure have the sole right to use the initials RD (récemment dégorgé).

6. All these wines are produced by a second fermentation in bottle and all, except one, have their own AOC. Crémant de Cramant is the odd man out as it has not got its own AC but comes under the AC of Champagne.

A bottle of the creaming (half-sparkling) wine from the vineyards of Cramant.

Many of us find the not fully sparkling wine of Cramant an ideal aperitif. There was a time when the bottle quite often carried no gold foil or wire cage. The cork (which was a normal champagne cork) was kept in position by a single metal clamp. It was an original package, but not acceptable to the public who thought the bottle looked naked and had somehow got through the bottling line without being properly dressed.

Crémant de Cramant is obviously euphonious, which may add to its attraction. It literally means 'Creaming from Cramant', the latter being a 100 per cent rated village in the Côte de Blancs, planted only for white grapes.

7. i. *Sekt* is the German word for sparkling wine. But the unqualified word *Sekt* on a German label may mean the wine has been produced in Germany, but from wines produced outside Germany.
ii. *Deutscher Sekt* (German Sekt) must be made only from German grapes, but need not be a *Qualität* wine, it can be a *Tafelwein*.
iii. *Deutscher Sekt BA* is their top quality and can only be produced from individual *Anbaugebiete* – not from blends of various *Anbaugebiete*.

8. The wine was Catawba sparkling wine. Catawba is a non-*vinifera*, native grape of America, of the family *Vitis labrusca*. Both Sillery and Verzenay are villages in the Montagne de Reims and each is rated 100 per cent for its black grapes. Presumably, in the last century, it was common to find the name Sillery or Verzenay on the label, but I have never seen it. Strictly theoretically, either name could be used for Champagne Blanc de Noirs or still red wine – Coteaux Champenois.

9. A bone dry champagne to which no *liqueur d'expedition* (sweetening) has been added.

10. Asti Spumante. Years ago, in the pre-ski lifts era, my family used to spend Christmas in Switzerland. On gala nights when the grown-ups drank champagne (right through the meal in those days) the young were allowed Asti – it is still low in alcohol, these days. Because of

this early introduction, one continued to assume that Asti Spumante was kids' stuff. It is not, definitely not.

It is a naturally sweet wine made from the Moscato grape (a high-sugar grape) in the Provinces of Piedmont, Asti, Cuneo and Alessandria, and of course it is sparkling, some people prefer the word 'bubbling'.

Some of us forget that Italians are large consumers of French champagne and indeed produce a number of 'champagne method' wines, but Asti is not considered a champagne style wine. Admittedly, it is sometimes made by the *méthode champenoise* but probably to its detriment. One of the essentials of Asti production is speed. The finished article must still retain all its youth and freshness and the taste of Moscato – one year from the grape to the glass is about the form achieved by the Charmat method. It is the typical conversation or pudding wine, at least so I always thought till the other day when we watched, fascinated, while two serious, business-suited men chose Asti to go with their steak. The restaurateur produced enormous glasses, which was later explained when a peach was placed in each. The peaches were spiked with a fork and the bubbles made them revolve.

11. In California where Domaine Chandon is the name of an elegant winery making stylish sparkling wines by the champagne method. Most are a blend of Chardonnay, Pinot Noir and Pinot Blanc and titled Brut; there is also a Blanc de Noir made with the white juice of Pinot Noir grapes. Chandon is owned by Moët-Hennessy who also own Moët et Chandon (and Hennessy cognac) in France.

12. It looks difficult and awkward but is in fact convenient and the traditional way of serving champagne and other sparkling wines. Champagne and similar bottles are thicker and heavier than a still-wine bottle as they have to withstand the pressure of the sparkle in the bottle. The thumb in the punt and the weight of the bottle balanced on the four fingers makes pouring even a magnum less tiring than the normal grip. Thumbs up for bubbly!

SECTION

III

Around the World

Wine Classics

1. Château Mouton Rothschild has 'declared a vintage' every year from 1945 to 1986 inclusive. True or false?

2. However prestigious a château in the Médoc may be, its AOC can only be one of eight. The leading four are Pauillac, Margaux, St Julien, and St Estèphe. Please name the remaining four.

3. The classified growths are those Bordeaux wines which were listed in the classification of 1855. Today, the purist now calls the classification of 1855 'the classification of 1855 and 1973'. Why should this be?

4. Few could name all the *Grosslagen* and *Einzellagen* of the Rheinland but which is the only *Bereich* of the Rheingau?

5. Which of the following wines would you normally expect to be the most expensive?
    (a) Le Montrachet
    (b) Bâtard-Montrachet
    (c) Puligny-Montrachet Les Combettes?

6. We were once told that when the owners of the superb Graves Château Haut Brion decided to make a small amount of white wines which eventually would prove to be amongst the finest and driest white Graves available, they bought their vines from Château Yquem who produce the world's greatest sweet wine. Perhaps the story is totally apocryphal, but it does raise a question. Is it normal for the same grape varieties to be able to make the driest or sweetest wines?

7. The oldest known wine quiz question is: 'How did the great Château Beychevelle of St Julien acquire its name?' No quiz would be complete without it – so have a go!

8. The cream of Burgundy comes from the Côte d'Or which is divided into a northern and southern Côte. What are they called?

9. Reputedly, the highest quality Burgundies are found in the Côte de Nuits (the northern section of the Côte d'Or). Do you agree?

10. Although Baron Philippe de Rothschild eventually achieved promotion for his beloved Château Mouton Rothschild from second growth to first growth, his other Château Mouton-Cadet still remains a third growth. Your comments please.

11. It is really a little strange that the traditional, classical wine area of Spain with a history of winemaking going back to Roman times, became classical primarily thanks to the French. Are we talking of Catalonia, Navarre or Rioja?

12. What is the significance of the word *classico* when applied to any Italian wine?

13. The Italian Château Yquem? Well it's doubtful that the Italians today would want to accept such a title, but *Botrytis* or no *Botrytis*, it is still a delightful Italian dessert wine. Please give:
    (a) The name
    (b) The place of origin

14. Can you name the vineyard financed by Denver oil money and noted for its exceptional quality wines?

15. A famous palace on a famous label (see photograph) – but what is the name of the wine?

Answers on page 112

Tour de France

1. Which commune *appellation* features most in the 1855 classification of the Médoc?

2. There are a number of British names long associated with the wines of Bordeaux – Lawton, Barton, Lynch, Brown and Talbot (or was it a Norman name?) being a few. Even so, it is particularly pleasing to think that St George is still honoured in Burgundy and Bordeaux. Can you please elucidate?

3. 'First growth whites are rare these days, except in the Côte Chalonnaise.'
True or false?

4. Northern red wine Burgundy is the land of the Pinot Noir and its southern area, the land of the Gamay grape. Is there any AC Bourgogne that can be made by blending wine of the Pinot Noir with wine of the Gamay. The question is somewhat esoteric.

5. Name the odd man/men out:
   (a) Aloxe-Corton
   (b) Corton Grancey
   (c) Corton
   (d) Corton Charlemagne

6. Côte Rôtie, Brouilly and Morgon are three AC red wines situated in the Department of the Rhône. True or false?

7. It is an accepted fact in Burgundy that, very often, a single geographical name denotes a higher *appellation* than a double-barrelled name. Chambolle-Musigny, for example, is a generic *appellation*, but Musigny is a *grand cru*.
   (a) How has this come about?
   (b) Can you think of similar examples?

8. Vouvray and Montlouis face each other across the Le Loir river. True or false?

9. Of the following northern Rhône areas, one produces AC red wine only, another AC white only and the third both AC red and white wines – which please is which? Hermitage, Côte Rôtie and Condrieu.

10. The brandies of France are also covered by the laws of AOC, or more accurately three brandies are. Please give their names.

11. The names of Graves and Entre-Deux-Mers suggest a similarity. Are the following comments true or false?
   (a) Both areas produce red and white wines.
   (b) Their white wines range from dry to sweet.

12. The two rivers Dordogne and Garonne meet together and flow into a third river. Can you name:
   (a) The third river?
   (b) The name of the wine area?

13. Bevy in the *Oxford Dictionary* means a large group. Put an acute accent on the 'e' and one can talk about a Bévy of fine wines – but from where?

14. Name the odd man out:
   (a) Château Grillet
   (b) Château Chalon
   (c) Châteauneuf-du-Pape.

15. A city which appears a curious blend of France and Germany. The clue is white wine probably served with goose liver. Can you name the city (see photograph) and the wine area of which it is the capital?

Answers on page 118

The Europeans

1. Slate is as important in the Mosel Valley as chalk is to Champagne. This is reflected in the names of a number of vineyard sites. Can you name three?

2. Continue along from Treviso (Veneto) and one comes to Venegazzu. What is this well known for?

3. What is your experience of white Chianti?

4. Brunello di Montalcino is:

  (a) Cheap wine from Piedmont
  (b) A treasure from Tuscany

Which is the more accurate description?

5. Most wine areas have their rivers. At Koblenz the Rhein throws off another major river which flows south-west. North of Trier, this river has a tributary and south of Trier another tributary, both highly important wine areas. Please name the major river and its two tributaries.

6. Strange that a Black Cockerel and a Pink Cherub can do the same job – at least in Tuscany. Can you elucidate?

7. Valpolicella has the largest production of red wines in the Veneto. Which DOC in the same area produces the most white wines?

8. What is probably the most popular of the Castelli Romani DOC wines?

9. What does the German word *Schloss* mean? Can you give the name of a vineyard in the Rheinhessen of the same name?

10. Name a DOC Italian wine discovered and nurtured by an Englishman and once the toast of the Royal Navy.

11. Barolo, Barbera, Barbaresco, Bardolino.

　(a) Do they all come from the same area of Italy?
　(b) Are any of them grape names?

12. Can any single wine *appellation* from anywhere in the world have two towns of such ancient historical fame as Siena and Florence within its very boundaries? What is the name of the *appellation*?

13. Which is the village? Which is the grape?

　(a) Spanna
　(b) Nebbiolo
　(c) Gattinara

14. Recioto della Valpolicella can be vinified dry when it is called what? or sweet when its description is what?

15. There are no records to suggest that Ali Baba visited Montilla-Moriles, but had he done so, why would he have felt comfortably 'at home'?

16. It is white, Italian and DOC. Its bottle is designed to remind one of a Greek–Roman amphora. Which wine are we talking of and from where exactly?

Answers on page 124

1. The *borracho* itself might well give you a headache, but not such a nasty one as you would get by drinking its contents. What is the clue?

2. Which Canadian Province drinks most wine per head?

3. Egri Bikaver: what does Egri mean?

4. Mavrud is one of the black grapes of Bulgaria, but have you heard the legend of Mavrud?

Near and Far

5. 'Really, I can't take their Cabernet Sauvignons – they are a one-glass wine.' About which wines do you imagine this rather extraordinary remark is being said?

6. The most popular wine in Greece is named not after a place, a grape, nor even a Saint. It is generic, coming in all forms other than sparkling. Its name and any comments.

7. Where in Canada are the majority of vineyards?

8. How would you describe a Canadian Liquor Control Board? People who have not visited Canada during the last ten or fifteen years had perhaps better not answer.

9. Familiarly known as Zin, and much beloved in one of the world's finest wine areas. What are we talking about?

10. Where is a Martini nothing to do with gin or vodka? Clue – the answer lies outside Italy.

11. Who christened what area 'John Bull's Vineyard'?

12. Whatever one writes about California is probably out of date before the ink dries. Even so the following grapes must still be among the most used varietals. Can you name their assumed area of origin?

(a) French Colombard
(b) Zinfandel
(c) Chenin Blanc
(d) Carignane
(e) Cabernet Sauvignon
(f) Barbera
(g) Grenache
(h) Ruby Cabernet
(i) Chardonnay
(j) Petite Sirah

13. Junipero Serra
Jean-Louis Vignes
Agoston Haraszthy
Davis
Where in the world are we?

14. A typical California vineyard with palms and vines intermixed. Can you name the famous valley where it is located, north of San Francisco?

Answers on page 130

Wine Classics

1. True. Château Mouton Rothschild has produced some wine under the Château label every year since the war and this may equally apply to every first growth red Bordeaux. This fact is a tremendous tribute to the advance in oenological knowledge. Certainly, little or no wine was produced by the major châteaux in those disastrous years of the thirties – 1930, 1931, 1932 and 1935. Today, the back-room persons (there must be about as many female wine chemists as male) understand and control what is going on from fermentation to bottling. We have to thank them for making no wine, or bad wine, a thing of the past.

2. Médoc
Haut Médoc
Moulis
Listrac

3. The purist only uses this heading when he wants (totally correctly) to show Château Mouton Rothschild as a *premier cru classé* (first growth). This Château was upgraded from second *cru* to first *cru* in 1973. The only alteration made since 1855.

4. Johannisberg: Johann commemorates the greatest of all Johns, berg is the hill on which the village stands.
   The German wine laws of 1971 laid down 11 areas where *Qualitätswein* would be produced called *Anbaugebiete* (see the answer to question 9 in *Tips of the Wine Trade*). These areas were subdivided into a *Bereich*, a large wine district. The *Bereich* was itself further divided into *Grosslagen*, a smaller area of similar vineyards. Each *Grosslage* forms an umbrella for *Einzellagen*, individual vineyards, each of which cannot be less than 12 acres and which are often controlled by a number of owners.
   Theoretically, and in practice, the highest quality wines are found amongst the *Einzellagen*, the next quality are *Grosslagen*, and the *Bereich* represents a general quality. The word *Bereich* may feature on the labels. The fact that a wine is a *Grosslage* or even an *Einzellage* is not allowed

A traditional Weintor *at cellars in Germany.*

to appear on the label. There is presumably some esoteric reason for such legislation but it is strange. There are roughly 150 *Grosslagen* and 2600 *Einzellagen* which are all indications of quality, and as far as the label is concerned this information is withheld from the public.

In Johannisberg, indeed in the Rheingau, one might be in the Médoc. Like the Médoc the great estates are all there although in a far more compact formation, and admittedly, the colour of the wine is different. One could easily visit three Schloss by bicycle during the day, but this would be unwise. At German tastings, a spittoon is not always available. It is a question of upbringing; some of us can taste with little sips others have to have the spittoon routine. Germans seem to prefer the sip technique. The Schloss Johannisberg, which arguably produces some of the highest quality Rieslings in the Rheingau, is awarded the right of an *Einzellage* as indeed is its neighbour Schloss Vollrads. Both Schloss use labels and particularly coloured capsules to show the different *'Prädikats'* of their wine. Their wines seem to complement each other, both are

113

totally classical, but Schloss Vollrads vinifies the Riesling with an austerity unique to itself and enjoyable to all. It is a little absurd, and indeed wrong, to compare only two Schloss in the Rheingau; it is well worth seeking out the wines of Von Simmern, Schloss Schönborn, Steinberg, Schloss Reinhartshausen, indeed of all the Rheingau.

Whatever other grapes may be grown in either the Rheingau or the Mosel-Saar-Ruwer one thinks only of Riesling. Do the two areas compare? That sort of question can only be answered by bottles, glasses and a spittoon or lots of bread.

In the great vintage years of Germany – which means Riesling years – the grapes of the Rheingau must still be riper than those of the Mosel. In lesser years, they are certainly riper. Therefore all the Rheingau produces stronger, fatter, rounder wines. And now for a really controversial remark. A great Rheingau wine for conversation, a great Mosel (perhaps from the Saar) with the fish.

5. Le Montrachet is universally acknowledged as the finest dry white wine world-wide. It is a *grand cru* in the communes of Puligny-Montrachet and Chassagne-Montrachet, as indeed is its neighbour and fellow *grand cru* Bâtard-Montrachet.

The old saying 'Unto him who hath shall be given ...' applies to many of the world's greatest wines. Once a wine has arrived at the top of its particular *appellation*, and in most years is therefore a certain sell, the owners can afford to produce it in a totally classical manner (which is the most expensive) and so keep it there, but of course the owners have to be dedicated vintners.

Puligny-Montrachet Les Combettes is a *premier cru* wine and on this occasion comes third in price. In certain years, and from certain suppliers, it could easily come top in any blind tasting of Côte de Beaune whites excluding Le Montrachet.

6. Yes. Grape variety does not necessarily determine the sweetness or dryness of the wine. Sweetness or dryness is decided by the style of vinification, soil and often the micro-climate.

Let us stick to Graves and Sauternes. The grapes

common to both are the Sauvignon, Semillon and some Muscadelle.

In northern Graves, the wines are normally vinified dry and the Sauvignon takes pride of place usually with some Semillon, but not always, and occasionally with a touch of Muscadelle.

As one travels south to the borders of Sauternes, the soil changes and rich (*moelleux*) Graves can be made. The grape percentages also change, the Semillon takes first place, the Sauvignon second and there is more Muscadelle in the blend.

When one reaches Sauternes and Barsac, a micro-climate plays an all-important role. In the early autumn (in ideal years), the mornings are damp and misty, but the afternoons bright and hot. These conditions bring on *Botrytis cinerea* (a fungus that may wreck your strawberry beds) but is a godsend to Sauternes.

But *Botrytis* doesn't play fair as it rarely, if ever at one go, affects a whole vineyard, scarcely even whole bunches of grapes, so picking the grapes in a vineyard affected by *Botrytis* is a lengthy performance. *Botrytis* grapes are shrivelled and raisin-like. Their sugar content is waterless and concentrated resulting in a high sugar must and an eventual high alcohol, very sweet wine. Only the greatest Sauternes/Barsac châteaux can afford to pick and constantly repick their vineyards, so that only *Botrytis* grapes are fermented for their main label. Equally only the greatest châteaux can be overselective when finalizing their blend. Remember, we are picking in mid-autumn when rain can happen at any time.

Many Sauternes châteaux will wait as long as they dare for the arrival of *Botrytis*, then carry out a normal harvest regarding any *Botrytis* they may have as a bonus.

Like southern Graves, Semillon is Sauterne's first grape with Muscadelle playing a larger part than in any other Bordeaux whites. But of course if you want to make Sauternes dry, nothing could be easier, except the AOC is forfeited. Simply pick before *Botrytis* has appeared and ferment the must totally.

7. To appreciate the story fully, one must have sat, during a fine evening, on the outside terrace of Château Bey-

chevelle (name dropping?) and watched the river Gironde across the vista of an ideal garden. Almost certainly the finest view in the Médoc.

We are told that, in the seventeenth century, the Grand Admiral of France lived hereabouts. As the ships sailed down the Gironde, each saluted the Admiral by lowering their sails, the French term for which is *'baissez les voiles'*. Over the years, this phrase became *'Beychevelle'*.

The story is substantiated by the 'boat' which is the background to the Château Beychevelle label and by the name of their second wine Réserve de l'Amiral.

8. The northern Côte is the Côte de Nuits, the southern Côte is the Côte de Beaune. Bearing in mind its world fame, the Côte d'Or is a tiny narrow vineyard stretching from Dijon to Chagny – 60 km.

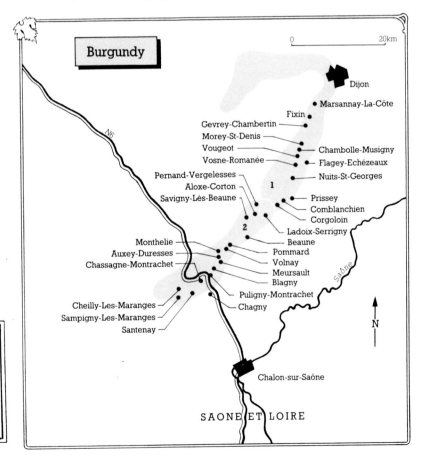

Wine Regions

1 Côte de Nuits
   (Côte d'Or)
2 Côte de Beaune
   (Côte d'Or)

9. Certainly not. The highest quality white Burgundies are found further south in the Côte de Beaune. If one accepts the concept that a *grand cru* Burgundy red or white is the best wine of its *appellation* over the years – and I think one must – the score card tells the story. All the red *grand crus* are in the Côte de Nuits except Le Corton and all the white *grand crus* are in the Côte de Beaune except Musigny which makes about 50 dozen bottles for the whole world, but still counts.

One is apt to get mesmerized by the white *grand crus* of the Côte de Beaune and forget there are seven white *grand crus* in Chablis whose prices are slightly nearer the earth.

10. Mouton-Cadet is of course neither a château nor a third growth, it is a branded Bordeaux wine. One assumes that much of the wine not considered good enough when the blend for the Mouton Rothschild label is finally agreed, goes into Mouton-Cadet. In theory, any AC red Bordeaux can legally make up Mouton-Cadet, reputedly the largest selling claret in the world. Baron Philippe also owns a fifth-growth château named Mouton-Baronne-Philippe in memory of his wife Pauline.

11. Rioja, in the province of Logroño in northern Spain. Wood ageing in small casks as practised in Bordeaux first attracted the Rioja winemakers at the end of the eighteenth century, but took an enormous leap forward when *Phylloxera* hit Bordeaux. Many of the Bordeaux merchants then crossed the border and sought safer vineyards where they could practise their wine skills. They preached and practised the ageing of wine in the Bordeaux *barriques* which became widely accepted by the Rioja vintners. Today, Rioja, Navarre and Catalonia offer wonderful value, notably in red wines, and bottle ageing is slowly gaining pride of place.

A Rioja wine will carry a back label stating one of four quality standards:

   i. *Garantia De Origen*
   ii. *Crianza*: one year minimum ageing in oak, three years from vintage to sale
   iii. *Reserva*: minimum two years in cask, one year in bottle

iv. *Gran Reserva*: minimum three years in cask, two years in bottle

Modern thinking is that some of the requirements for ageing in cask can be exchanged for ageing in bottle.

12. *Classico* does not mean that the wine must be of higher quality than the same DOC not labelled *classico*. It means that the wine is made from grapes grown in the *classico* area of Valpolicella, Chianti or wherever. The *classico* area is the original area which over the years has been extended. The 'new' vineyards receive the same DOC but not the magic addition *classico*. One assumes the original of anything must be the best and this applies probably to most of the Italian *classico* wines, but it seems unfair that vineyards (with the same DOC) outside the *classico* area cannot earn the title *classico* by achieving the required quality.

13. (a) Picolit, which is also the name of the grape
(b) Colli Orientali del Friuli

14. Jordan winery, created by a Denver geologist in imitation of the finest Bordeaux châteaux, planting Cabernet Sauvignon and Merlot and using both classic and modern winemaking techniques in luxurious surrounds. In the Alexander Valley of California, near the Pacific Ocean, the climate is marvellous for grapes. The first wine was made in 1976 and was recognized as very fine; now Jordan wines are collectors' items – Chardonnay is also available.

15. Mateus Rosé from Portugal, one of the greatest names in the world of rosé.

Jordan Vineyard and Winery is organized in the manner of a Bordeaux château.

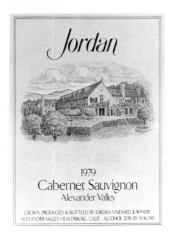

II

Tour de France

1. The score is Margaux, 21 châteaux; Pauillac, 18; St Julien, 11; and St Estèphe, 4.

One learns at an early age that for breed and elegance one chooses Margaux and Pauillac, although not necessarily in that order; that the greatest Pauillac outlives all other areas; that for fullness and vinosity St Estèphe is one's choice; and that probably for people like you and me, the wines of St Julien are the easiest to drink. Like platitudes, all these types of sayings are based on truth and frankly can be of help if one is trying to name a wine. But so often (thank goodness) the average wine-lover has his favourite wines for totally personal reasons. Château Gruaud-Larose Faure 1924 (there used to be two châteaux, Faure and Sarget) was the first claret I am conscious of drinking and, to this day, I am biased towards Château Gruaud-Larose. For totally unimportant reasons, I am equally biased towards Château Léoville Poyferré, but obviously am fully aware that in the open market Château Léoville-Las Cases invariably fetches the higher price.

2. In Burgundy, Les St Georges is one of the first growth vineyards of Nuits-St-Georges.

In Bordeaux, St Georges is one of the northern communes which can add St Emilion to its name to form the AC St-Georges-St-Emilion.

3. True. The Côte Chalonnaise, perhaps now more often referred to as the Mercurey Region, is the southern extension of the Côte de Beaune. Its main wines are:

Mercurey:	primarily red
Givry:	primarily red
Rully:	primarily white
Montagny:	all white and for some reason all first growth.

We understand Montagny, which can be truly Chardonnay, can only be first growth if the wine is not less than 11.5 per cent alcohol, but our understanding is also that the AC Montagny cannot be given to the appropriate wines unless they are 11.5 per cent alcohol! Easy isn't it?

4. Yes. But anyone who quotes Bourgogne Passe-Tout-Grains is, alas, wrong. This latter wine is a blend of grapes, two-thirds Gamay with one-third Pinot Noir which are vinified together. It is not made from blending two wines. AC Bourgogne can be produced by blending Pinot Noir with any of the nine *cru* Beaujolais. They are all 100 per cent Gamay and can all be declassified to Bourgogne.

119

5. Aloxe-Corton, Corton and Corton Charlemagne are AC Burgundy wines. Corton Grancey is a prestigious brand of the House of Latour who have cellars in Corton. As a brand, it is the odd man out.

Of the three wines, only Corton Charlemagne is a white *appellation* only, and is therefore the odd man out, as the *appellations* Aloxe-Corton and Corton cover red and white wines; in practice, appreciably more red.

6. True. Côte Rôtie is an important quality wine in the north of the Rhône wine area, made from Syrah grapes tempered with some white Viognier. Brouilly and Morgon are both Beaujolais (grape, Gamay Noir à Jus Blanc). Many of us have to be reminded that most of the Beaujolais area is in the Department of the Rhône. Beaujolais labels may well show the bottler as apparently having his cellars in the Rhône which puzzles people. It is correct as long as one remembers it is the Department of the Rhône, not the Rhône wine area.

7. (a) It came about for an almost human reason. The original village of Chambolle took pride in adding the

The charming old Château of Gevrey-Chambertin in the Côte de Nuits, whose vineyards produce fine red wines of the same name.

120

name of its greatest vineyard (its greatest son) Musigny to its own.

(b) Other examples are:

> Aloxe-Corton – generic; Corton – *grand cru*
> Chassagne-Montrachet – generic; Montrachet – *grand cru*
> Gevrey-Chambertin – generic; Chambertin – *grand cru*

Perhaps the Chambolle-Musigny example is the most spectacular, the generic *appellation* may produce at one vintage around 45 000 cases, while Musigny produces less than 3000.

8. False, sorry but of course they face each other across La Loire – not the little Le Loir. Both wines are made from the Chenin Blanc grape.

9. Hermitage: equally fine red and white wine, but far more red

Côte Rôtie: only AC red

Condrieu: only AC white

10. i. In the slightly wild Department of Gers (south-east of Bordeaux) one finds a slightly wild brandy – Armagnac.
ii. Calvados du Pays d'Auge: the geographical addition 'du Pays d'Auge' is obligatory to earn the AOC. This distillation of apples, pears or both comes from Normandy, an area of chic and cheese – Deauville and Pont l'Éveque.
iii. Cognac: to many, the fairest brandy of them all, but even so the oft-given description of *'digestif'* seems to be stretching it a bit. Both Armagnac and cognac are made only from white grapes and both use, amongst others, St Emilion, Folle Blanche, and Colombard.

An enjoyable moment happened recently in Cognac, when we were tasting vintage cognacs of a single year in the *paradis* of a famous House who store such brandies in barrels for use in their blends. The young Frenchman conducting the affair discreetly enquired our various ages with a view to letting us taste a brandy from the date of our birth. I was anxious to taste the famous 1900 and so gave that date as my birth. The Frenchman did a slight double-take but nothing more – until we left the cellar. He then, totally seriously and with gentle solicitude, took my arm and offered to help me down the steps. The French had won 'game, set and match'!

It may seem strange that a distillation of apples/pears should be a brandy. Most of us regard the latter as a distillation of wine. However (unless it has recently been changed), the EEC have not yet defined brandy. One hopes it will eventually be given the classification *Eaux de Vie du Vin*.

11. (a) False; there is no AC red Entre-Deux-Mers. Red wines made here are called Bordeaux Supérieur. Certainly, the Graves area produces red and white wines, indeed their red AC wines are normally of higher quality than their white wines.
(b) False: AC Entre-Deux-Mers white wines have to be dry. AC Graves produce white wines from the driest to the sweetest. But the classified château white Graves in the north of the area are all dry.

12. (a) The river Gironde
    (b) Bordeaux
The join of the Dordogne and Garonne has the reputation of reminding one of the tail of a swallow.

13. Bévy is a village in the Hautes Côtes de Nuits in Burgundy. Thanks to Maison Geisweiler et Fils, the ancient vineyard area of Hautes Côtes de Nuits, which for various reasons had petered out, is once more in full bearing. The grapes are the classical Burgundian duo of Pinot Noir and Chardonnay. The wines of Bévy, we are told, are not for long bottle ageing and are elegant rather than robust.

14. Château Grillet, because it is a private estate and not a commune or a town. Château Grillet (a tiny appellation AOC) produces rare white wine in northern Rhône from the Viognier grape.
    Château Chalon is the AOC for the rather strange *'vin jaune'* and is a commune in the Jura country. Basically, *vin jaune* is a yellowish colour and tastes like unfortified

sherry. The wine (Savagnin grape) is left on ullage in wood for a minimum of six years, but develops *flor*, as in Jerez, which seals it against total oxidation. It is less expensive to stick to sherry.

Châteauneuf-du-Pape was a new château built near Avignon in the fourteenth century by a new French Pope Clement V. Pope Clement was previously Archbishop of Bordeaux and would probably have enjoyed the fact that

The medieval palace at Avignon, once occupied by a succession of French popes.

the site of his château (now a charming country town) is also the best-known wine of southern Rhône. Châteauneuf-du-Pape is a strong southern wine which needs ageing both in wood and bottle to give of its best, and its best is worth the wait.

The soil in that part of France is strange in that it is covered in large stones. In some Châteauneuf-du-Pape vineyards, it is difficult to believe that the large round pebbles have not been carefully placed there which, indeed, they have, but by nature. They have the helpful effect of generating and holding extra heat.

15. Strasbourg is the city and of course Alsace the wine region.

The Europeans

1. The key word is *'Lay'* meaning slate – or does it? At a recent seminar, a student got up and assured us *'Lay'* did not mean slate in German. He was born German, his first language was German and the word for slate was ... then came something that sounded like a gutteral oath. Anyhow right or wrong to a Mosellen, *Lay* equals slate, and, in that part of the world, slate holds the heat of the sun and warms the vineyards at night. Occasionally storms cause the slate to go crashing down the hillside and the sturdy Mosellen or his *Frau* carry it back. Much of the Mosel vineyard area is totally precipitous. Small tractors may be used on cables, and life has become slightly easier by roads having recently been built across the mountain. But still most work is done by people standing on the steepest of slopes and one is amazed that over the years this has not caused an emergence of humans with one leg appreciably shorter than the other. A few examples of vineyards are:
Grosslagen – Munzlay, Beerenlay and Kurfurstlay
Einzellagen – Sonnenlay, Rotlay and Kirchlay

2. One of the great red wines of Italy. It is made in the Bordeaux style and obviously therefore is not DOC. The

grape varieties (need one say) are Cabernet Sauvignon and Franc, Merlot and Malbec. Their ageing is in small oak wood. One can equally find there a charming non-DOC, dry white wine, predictably made from the Chardonnay.

There is a DOC covering other wines in the district, *Montello e Colli Asolani*, which rather curiously allows the use of Cabernet, Merlot and Malbec.

3. Alas, no such wine exists. However, a few years back the Chianti producers came up with the most modern of white wines called Galestro which, one is told, is dialect for the local soil – Trebbiano grape, cold fermentation, no wood, slight tingle, rigid dry, low in alcohol and (to many of us) low in appeal. The *classico* growers also had a shot at a white wine called Bianco della Lega, but we've never met. Perhaps the most satisfying white DOC Tuscan wine is the Vernaccia Di San Gimignano. Elsewhere in Italy, notably in Umbria, their white wines are constantly showing improved and more modern qualities.

4. Brunello from Montalcino in Tuscany and vinified from the Sangiovese Grosso grape is a DOCG Italian wine and indeed a treasure. One is told in the Rome wine shops that an old Brunello Riserva will fetch the price of any of the greatest Bordeaux. A few years ago, it was almost impossible to find a great Italian wine outside Italy and certainly most of us have little or no idea how to serve them, even today. The great Italian wines really need age in bottle – the sort of age that must make them very expensive and then people tend to buy something they know more about. High quality Italian wines are a mystery except to the very lucky initiated few.

5. The major river is the Mosel. The northern tributary is the Ruwer and the tributary south of Trier is the Saar. In ripe years, the Rieslings of the Saar can produce some of Germany's finest wines. The whole area (*Anbaugebiet*) is known as 'Mosel-Saar-Ruwer'.

6. They are both the emblems of Tuscan Consorzi. Long before the DOC laws were introduced by the Italian government in 1963, there existed wine communities (*Con-*

sorzi) made up of local winemakers who formed, as it were, a club to protect the quality and integrity of their local wines in every possible way. They had one excellent idea which even the DOC does not have today. The wine of all the members had to be pretasted before a numbered neck band – issued by the *consorzio* – could be fixed to the top of the bottle in such a way that the cork could not be drawn without breaking the *consorzio*'s neck band. The weak point of all *consorzi* was that membership was voluntary and thus non-members were not subjected to the same controls. Since the advent of DOC and DOCG, membership of the *consorzi* is decreasing, particularly among the larger shippers.

The Black Cockerel is the emblem of the *consorzio* which represents the Chianti *classico* members, while the Pink Cherub (*putto*) represents the six similar surrounding areas in the hills of Arentini, Senesi, Fiorentini, Pissani, Montelbano and Rufina.

Now for a complete *non sequitur*, but still hopefully of interest to the wine crowd. It was the reference to a Black

The black cockerel familiar in the Chianti classico area.

Rooster that brought it to mind. Anyone visiting Rioja (Spain) should try and stay at the Parador at Santo Domingo de la Calzada which is 47 km from Logroño. There is an interesting church in the village and immediately above one's head on entering is an elaborate carved wooden cage housing permanently a live rooster which constantly takes part in the service.

7. Soave, made primarily from the Garganega grapes plus, of course, Trebbiano. Like Valpolicella, it can appear as *recioto*, *classico*, *superiore* or sparkling.

8. Frascati. It is also usually the carafe wine in the better Rome fish restaurants. But beware – it was our first day in Rome and we were full of the joys of spring, so we ordered a large carafe which turned out to be $1\frac{1}{2}$ litres. The waiter knew we had made a mistake and was expecting to finish it off himself – no way!

Barolo is one of only five Italian wines that has been awarded the valued DOCG.

9. The word *Schloss* means castle. Oppenheimer Schloss in the *Grosslage* of Krötenbrunnen within the *Bereich* of Nierstein.

10. Marsala, a fortified dessert wine from Sicily. The credit of 'discovering' Marsala is given to the Woodhouse brothers – at the end of the eighteenth century. They were soon supplying Nelson's fleet, and its popularity in England arrived in the last century via the Navy. The wine is sherry-like or Madeira-like, dry or sweet, young or old. To get the *appellation* 'Solera Riserva', the wine must be aged not less than ten years. One wonders if there is any other wine which has to age ten years before earning a descriptive *appellation*. For the cooking experts, it is also the base for Zabaglione.

11. (a) They all come from Piedmont except Bardolino, which is in the Veneto.

Barolo and Barbaresco complement each other. Both are among the greatest wines of Italy, but if Barolo is Italy's Chambertin, Barbaresco is her Musigny and basically easier to get on with. Barolo we are told needs oxidation, open it the night before, don't drink it all at once, leave some for friends the next day. It makes ordering it in a restaurant complicated. Bardolino is an entirely different kettle of fish, and comes from the shores of Lake Garda. It is similar to Valpolicella and is vinified from the same grape varieties of Corvina, Rondinella and Molinara.

(b) Barbera is the name of the grape, but the DOC is never given to the grape, it is always geographical. The first Barbera of Piedmont is Barbera d'Alba, but the more popular and more elegant wine is the Barbera d'Asti.

12. The wine of course is Chianti, which since 1984 is DOCG.

Chianti, the very breath of Italy, has long ago grown up, and today rarely appears in a grass skirt. The Fiaschi have given way to a Bordeaux style bottle, often tinged with brown to withstand the sun's rays. Today, many Chiantis, *classico* or indeed from any region, are vinified to be laid down and aged.

The grape varieties remain the same, but the previous over-use of white grapes is universally less. They are primarily the black grapes Sangiovese plus some Canaiolo and the white Trebbiano – in the *classico* area, the very maximum is 5 per cent but usually less is used.

The *Governo* system (*Governo All'Uso Toscano*) is allowed within the *appellation*, but seems to be dying out. It involves refermenting the new wine during the winter months which facilitates the completion of the malolactic fermentation and creates glycerine, thus making the wine easier to drink young, particularly if one likes it a bit prickly on the tongue.

It will always be debated whether it was wise to grant the whole enormous area of Chianti the same top *appellation*, *Denominazione di Origine Controllata e Garantita*, but one must remember all DOCG wines are taste-tested before being granted the DOCG and certainly in 1984 (a modest year) many fell by the wayside.

13. (a) Spanna is the local name given by the Piedmontese for their noble black grape Nebbiolo.
(b) Cross the road into Lombardy and Nebbiolo/Spanna

becomes Chiavennasca – easy isn't it?

(c) Gattinara is yet one more fine DOC Piedmont red wine whose vineyards (mostly Nebbiolo) lie around the village of Gattinara.

14. The dry version is Amarone (fermented right through), a truly enormous wine.

The sweet version Amabile is voluptuous, and served at the end of the usual magnificent Italian repast to accompany some startling dessert is quite an endurance test.

Both Recioto della Valpolicella Amarone and Amabile get their muscle and high alcohol by allowing the grapes to wither and concentrate their sugar until the end of January with vinification following in February. The grapes involved are the well-known Veneto trio – Corvina, Rondinella and Molinara.

The word Recioto apparently means only the ears of the vines are picked – *recie* being a slang word for ear. I am a bit puzzled as to which part of the vine that is, but presumably it ripens more than the rest.

15. Because the wines of Montilla are fermented in huge *'Tinajas'*, giant clay Ali Baba-like containers. Why? is a good question. Similar 'urns' are used in Valdepeñas. Why? is equally a good question.

Montillas are as near as can be to unfortified sherry, but perhaps one should say, with Montillas, fortification is optional. *Finos* and *amontillados* are not fortified, *olorosos* may be. Their dark sweet dessert wines surely are.

Cordoba, the heart of Montilla, lies inland about 150 km north-east of Jerez. There are no sea breezes, it is very hot country. The soil of both areas is the same Albariza, but Montilla uses the Pedro Ximénez, whereas Jerez uses the Palomino grape reserving the PX for sweetening wines. In the hot Cordoban plain, the Pedro Ximénez produces a high sugar must and so a high alcohol wine which makes fortification not totally necessary.

Once the Montilla wines start their ageing process in oak barrels, the *criadera/solera* system of Jerez takes over, plus of course a natural production of the bacteria *'flor'*. One suspects that the regular drinkers of Montilla find

their taste more different from sherry than their method of production.

16. The wine is Verdicchio made primarily from the white grape of the same name. The area of production is The Marches which is bordered by the Adriatic in north-east Italy. Verdicchio is traditionally bottled in an amphora-style bottle. This may upset the purist but 'never judge a book by its cover'. Rather curiously, there are two DOC Verdicchios. Internationally, the more popular is Verdicchio Dei Castelli di Jesi. My bet goes to Verdicchio di Matelica (the emphasis is on the second syllable) as it bears the prettiest name in the wine bibliography. Both wines are produced in the Province of Ancona whose capital is a very fancy boat-building centre.

Near and Far

1. The clue is Madeira. The question is very dated, as the custom is certainly rare today, but was in full swing not so long ago with plenty of photos to prove it. The *borracho* is a goat's skin. The wine farmer would fill the *borracho* with the current year's wine and trek down the hills to sell to the Madeira wine producers in Funchal or wherever. The farmer would tie the *borracho* across his forehead with its two front legs and let the wine-filled goat skin lie down his back.

Madeira has been, and can again be, one of the greatest fortified wines of the world. It has almost been allowed to disappear but Portugal's membership of the EEC might see a revival. We are told her best customer is France where it is shipped in bulk, blended with culinary herbs and sold for *'la cuisine'*.

To find a single year vintage Madeira today is extremely difficult, but the Madeira Wine Company made a rare 1983 Terrantez, which should be well worth a trial taste in the middle of the next century – but such is vintage Madeira.

Quality Madeiras today go in for varietal grape labelling. Not so long ago perhaps, the grape name on the label represented only a style, but not today.

The most noble varieties are given below. They are all white and any bottle so labelled will contain at least 85 per cent of the named variety plus the local black grape Tinta Negra Mole.

Sercial:	The grape of the dry aperitif
Bual:	The grape making a sweet luscious dessert wine
Verdelho:	Slightly the Palo Cortado of Madeira, rich on the palate with a dry farewell
Malmsey:	Bual plus from the rich Malvasia dessert grape

All Madeira is fortified. The fermentation is sometimes stopped (as in port) for the sweeter wines by brandy, or the brandy is added later after fermentation.

An essential process in the production of, and totally peculiar to, Madeira is the *'estufagem'*. The young wines are 'baked' in an *estufa* (a heated area) for around six months. Heating the wine in this manner, which is certainly highly beneficial to it, is said to replace accurately the great advantages the wine used to have as casks of it were sailed across the Atlantic or Indian oceans.

2. This is almost a joke question, it has to be Quebec – but it is not. British Columbia wins first, Quebec second and Ontario third. But British Columbia drinks almost twice as much of their own wine as against those imported from outside Canada.

3. My understanding is that the letter 'i' at the end of a Hungarian word means 'from', therefore the meaning is 'from Eger'. A similar example is the Hungarian wine Szekszardi which comes from Szekszard.

As we all know, Egri Bikaver is the best known red wine of Hungary – 'Bull's Blood'. But Eger (incidentally an enchanting town) also produces a quality white wine from the Leanyka grape – 'Egri Leanyka' – and a number of these Hungarian grapes have dashing names, Leanyka means 'young girl'.

Other Hungarian grapes have attractive names such as Hárslevelü (linden leaf) and Szurkebarat (grey friar).

A Cabernet Sauvignon from the garden of the Balkans, Bulgaria.

4. The Mavrud legend tells of the intrepid youth who overcomes an impassable moat, the King's bodyguard and the King's daughter – only the last with co-operation. The King is as astonished as his daughter that one young man can achieve so much. All is finally forgiven when it is discovered that the youth had been reared, not on milk, but on the local Mavrud wine and everyone hiccups happily ever after.

Bulgaria is the garden of the Balkans. Flowers (primarily roses), fruit and vegetables grow there in great abundance, and *vinifera* grapes are no exception. It would be nice, but perhaps stupid, to think that Bulgaria had an old-world approach to winemaking; that red wines made from the local grapes, Mavrud and Gamza, and white wines from their grapes, Hemus and Dimiat, would be as popular world-wide as at home, but that is not the case. Bulgaria's approach to winemaking is modern and professional and geared to the export markets. Like many countries, their approach is varietal labelling (i.e. according to grape variety), and their vineyards are increasingly planted with the names everyone knows. They offer today fully acceptable wines from the noble varieties – Cabernet, Riesling, Merlot and Chardonnay – and suddenly Bulgaria has become a world exporter.

5. California Cabernets, be they from Napa, Santa Barbara or wherever. The remark itself is meant to suggest that after a sniff and a few sips, one knows exactly what one is drinking. The bouquet and taste of the grape comes over too strongly, the wine is too obvious and lacks subtlety. Such 'clever' remarks are not meant to be taken too seriously. They are carelessly let fall when the conversation flags and cause the odd explosion, but they still (rather annoyingly) can have a grain of truth.

In Bordeaux (where they play games occasionally) I confidently and wrongly named a wine Californian solely because the message of Cabernet Sauvignon was so obvious – it could be the other way round next time.

Anyhow, as we all know, many Californian vintners are now aiming to make their fine Cabernet Sauvignons with greater elegance and delicacy – in a word, more complex. But please, not too complex. The Californian climate can produce the ripest grapes on earth, and many of us love to sip our wine and immediately receive warm greetings from the grape.

6. The name is Retsina – a wine flavoured with resin. Folklore has it that when wines were formerly transported in goatskins, they were apt to taste of the innards of the goat. However, coating the goat container with resin miraculously gave the wine extra breed and bouquet. The more likely explanation is that resin was used as a closure floating on top of the wine in an amphora or similar earthenware vessel. More factually, resinated wines are very popular in many parts of southern Europe and can be addictive.

7. The Okanagan valley in the Province of British Columbia and the Niagara Peninsula in the Province of Ontario. The climates of both areas make the growing of *vinifera* grapes hazardous and not really commercial. Even so, all wineries produce some 100 per cent *vinifera* wines but in small quantities, notably the Cottage (Boutique) wineries – their *vinifera* white wines can be totally successful.

For table wines, the local *labrusca* is a forgotten grape and the principal plantings are European hybrids. Again overall, the white wines seem to have the higher quality.

Perhaps the next statement is out of place as it is not possible to prove, but if one had to name the country whose wines in the last five years have improved most, Canada must be in the running. The cynic of course will say 'Maybe, but from a low base!'

Yet everything seems set for a breakthrough. Most winemakers are Davis or highly trained European oenologists and the wineries have proved (most notably in BC) that *vinifera* can be grown, but certainly not at a price to compete with the usual *vinifera* vineyards – as yet.

The general set-up in both Provinces is that of the large firms who produce something of everything – fortified, table and Canadian 'champagne', bag in box or tetra-brik. There are then the table-wine-only firms, and finally the Cottage wineries dedicated mostly to cultivating the *vinifera*.

The selection of hybrid varieties is wide. Among the reds are Chelois, De Chaunac and Foch; among the whites are the Okanagan Riesling, Seyval Blanc and Dutchess.

8. In Canada, the sale of all alcohol is controlled by the Government and each Provincial Government has its own Liquor Control Board or Commission or Corporation, the names vary slightly, but the principles are the same. They control the stores which sell alcoholic products and they totally control the importation of all alcohol. A few years ago, the above statement would have been 100 per cent accurate. Today, in a few of the larger Provinces, there are elements of privatization. Not many years ago, the average selection of wines and spirits offered by a Province had not kept pace with the general advance in 'worldly affairs' of the people of the Province. But far worse was the quality of the shops. They seemed based on some rather Dickensian Post Office. One wrote out one's order and handed it through a grille.

Today, the change is complete; most stores are self-service, many are very large, with long hours of opening.

But the other side of the fence is always greener. One can't shop around, one can't get quantity discounts. If one lives in Toronto, the Buffalo wine stores seem to have a greater and cheaper selection of first growths. Those who live on the West Coast are tempted by Seattle, etc.

It is too academic to argue the pros and cons of a state liquor monopoly, the very word monopoly being out of favour today. Even so, they mostly study the public far more than the public realize. If anyone wants any drink not listed by the Province, so long as the order is not less than a dozen bottles, the Province is required to obtain it. This encourages the formation of serious wine groups whose members feel they are doing something better by buying a brand not listed by the Province.

9. The black grape variety Zinfandel and, wherever it came from, to a Californian (and indeed to most other people) it is the Californian grape.

One of the great attractions of the Californian vintners is that in addition to the large commercial concerns, an extremely wide spectrum of humanity is to be found. They could be ex-teachers from Davis, or successful businessmen who want to get away from it all or, indeed, others blessed with inherited wealth, or perhaps nothing, but who now work 12 hours a day to produce a better wine than their neighbours. They are mostly extroverts-plus, highly intelligent and dedicated. At times they behave like a kid with a new toy and experiment endlessly. The length of wood maturation and indeed the type of wood is almost a fetish. Late harvesting and long fermentation on the skins, all play their part – and certainly with Zinfandel.

Zinfandel stars as an enchanting young soubrette or an overweight Wagnerian opera singer. As a soubrette, it may be vinified to have the light freshness of a *primeur*, but in its operatic role it may reach around 16° alcohol and be as black as your hat. A warning to the over sixties – if you buy the richest of Zinfandels and expect to drink it yourself, you have an absurd over-estimation of the life-span of mankind!

10. In the Napa Valley of California, where the Louis M. Martini winery has been established since 1923 making mainly red wines such as Cabernet Sauvignon, Barbera and Zinfandel. The majority of the wines made here are intended for early consumption although some are 'special bottlings' intended for laying down. They also make a range of white wine varietals including Chardonnay and Gewürztraminer.

11. At the beginning of the nineteenth century, Napoleon's spies are reputed to have got thoroughly overexcited about the vineyards appearing in South Australia and christened them John Bull's Vineyards – not a very likely story.

Vines were first transported from Europe to Australia in the late eighteenth century. It is easy to forget that viticulture there is not something new, but the quality of their table wines (now in exportable quantities) is.

Not so long ago, one can remember bulk shipments of heavy red wines, full of iron and often used as a base for tonic wines or sold maybe as Australian Burgundy. Incidentally, if those wines were kept in bottle they improved faster than any red wine normally available.

There were also enormous 'ports' from the Barossa valley and certainly still are. They may be designed for something more serious but they taste wonderful outdoors on any sporting occasion. From a very early stage, there were 'flor' sherries and of course there was beer.

Then, hey presto, one began hearing about the skills of Australian oenologists, of their early practice of cold closed fermentation and their experiments with the 'bag in the box'. Two things have not changed: the climate (every year's a vintage year) and geographically, the areas of production. No doubt what those areas offer the wine-

Vineyard workers in the Barossa Valley, South Australia, in the mid-nineteenth century.

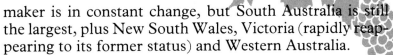

maker is in constant change, but South Australia is still the largest, plus New South Wales, Victoria (rapidly reappearing to its former status) and Western Australia.

As far as I know, there are still no laws of *appellation*, but you can read on the main and back labels exactly what you are drinking. Today, it may be Cabernet tempered with Merlot or Shiraz tempered with Cabernet. It may be Muscat vinified as an aperitif/dessert wine (curious how in every country sweet wines so often serve as both) or a 'sherry'.

Riesling can be any Australian white wine and it may be Semillon or Hunter, Clare or Rhein Riesling. But the most recent prize-winners have been their Chardonnays.

The French spies could obviously foretell the future.

12. (a) Cognac
   (b) Origin not certain, best bet Italy
   (c) Loire valley
   (d) Primarily Provence
   (e) Bordeaux
   (f) Piedmont
   (g) Southern Rhône
   (h) A Davis cross of Cabernet Sauvignon and Carignane
   (i) Burgundy and Champagne: one should really place the areas the other way round; there is surely more Chardonnay grown in Champagne than Burgundy!
   (j) Take your choice; it is certainly northern Rhône either as Syrah or Duriff; the latter has disappeared but was probably a poor relation of the Syrahs

Perhaps Pinot Noir should now be added to the above. There is something very special about the Pinot Noir, unless it is treated with tender loving care, one never knows what it is going to do next. Thanks to the rustic rapport with Burgundy and cherishing charm from Champagne, it gives its all. There are now plenty of signs of a successful courtship in California.

Finally, so many European grape varieties have been introduced to California, so many clones and crosses developed, and certain names abandoned as non-sellers, that the grape scene is confused. Here are a few of the anomalies:

i. Pinot Chardonnay is a misnomer; the grape is Chardonnay
ii. Pinot St Georges is a red *vinifera* and possibly an ancient Burgundian cross of Pinot Noir and Gamay à Jus Coloré
iii. Riesling in its German form is marketed as Johannisberg Riesling. Also used is the Grey Riesling thought by many not to be a Riesling at all but the Chauché Gris of France.
iv. Emerald Riesling is a California cross of Johannisberg Riesling and Muscadelle
v. Gamay Beaujolais is now thought to be a misnomer, and is probably a clone of Pinot Noir
vi. Fumé Blanc; a very marketable name for Sauvignon Blanc
vii. Gamay or Napa Gamay is thought to be the true descendant of the Gamay Noir à Jus Blanc

13. These four names have each played a part in the growth of the Californian wine picture. The oenology branch of the University of California very much continues to do so.

One can rarely pinpoint the actual start of any great undertaking. Over a period of time, they usually emerge slowly. The Franciscan monk, Junipero Serra (a very splendid name) is remembered, as he planted what was known as the 'Mission' grape in the various missions as they spread from San Diego (California) north to Sonoma. All this in the 1770s. Junipero surely had no thought or, indeed, wish to prove that California was ideal wine country. He merely wanted wine for sacramental purposes and, one hopes, the refectory table.

Over 50 years later, when the missions were secularized and their vineyards lay in disarray, business took over in the form of Jean-Louis Vignes.

It seems almost too good to be true that there was a man named Vignes, that he was a Bordelais, and that vines were his consuming interest, but so it was. At this very early stage, Vignes realized the wine potential of California and imported vines from his home country France. Both they and the Vignes family flourished. Perhaps Vignes started the influx into California of the major European wine interests which today continues unabated. As Junipero had proved, the Mission grape grew easily in California, so Vignes proved that the same applied to the noble *vinifera* grapes of Europe.

The scene is thus set for the emergence of Agoston Haraszthy. His name might suggest light opera, but he certainly landed a job that many of us would envy. During the 1860s he was assigned by the Governor of California to swan around Europe and collect every type of vine he thought suitable for Californian planting. Agoston arrived home with endless cuttings of *vinifera* varieties. Today, only *vinifera* vines may be planted for the wines of California. (However, they must be grafted on to American rootstock against *Phylloxera* as in Europe.)

The oenology branch of the University of California at Davis has been of great benefit to the whole wine world, but obviously most particularly to the vintners of California. Amongst many things, Davis has established five temperature zones suitable for wine grape growing. Each region is determined by the heat summation occurring in the zone. In simplistic terms, given a formula, one can work out the heat summation in those areas of Europe where the European grape varieties now being grown in California, best flourish. Having got this information, one can plant such varieties in the areas climatically best suited to them. Again, in simple terms, the grapes for light table wine fare better in the cooler coast regions while grapes for fortified wines can cope with the hotter inland sites.

At the moment, it must be true to say that Europe still chooses its quality wines by geography, while California chooses by grape variety, with the winemaker a close second.

14. The Napa Valley – said to be an Indian word meaning 'plenty'.

Illustration Acknowledgments

Jordan Vineyard and Winery	118
Richard Kihl	47, 49, 78
John Lipitch Associates	33 (above), 34
Mateus Rosé, Oporto	105
Moët et Chandon (London) Limited	69
H Parrot & Company Limited	75, 98-9, 126
Rainbird Publishing Group Ltd	62, 109, 120, 130
The Wine Club, Reading, Berkshire	6, 13, 18, 21, 33 (below), 36, 45, 52, 60, 64, 67, 71, 77, 82, 87, 90, 98 (below), 99, 101, 107, 111, 113, 123, 127, 132, 136

The maps and artwork were
drawn by Robert Mathias

140

INDEX